50

Profitable Business Ideas

You can start from home today...
... With Little or No Money

Includes Simple Step by Step Instructions

Ian Walker

Table Of Contents

Introduction

Do You Have a Dream?

Do you know what it is that you want to do in life? What is your dream? Your passion? Your life is too precious to do something that simply pays the bills, that is all right, or merely tolerable. **Unfulfilled dreams are demoralising and the cause of so much pain in the world.** As the song goes: "you've got to have a dream."

Ideally you should make money out of your dream, but the purpose of life on earth is for you to be *happy*. Money becomes less important if you are doing something that you truly love. Yes it's true, happiness is far more important than money and money cannot *buy* happiness. I am not discrediting money, I LOVE IT, but your happiness should be your number one priority. And the very best result is to be engaged in something you love doing, which *also* makes you a stack of loot!

Also your dream does not have to be meaningful to anybody but *you*. That is, if renovating a rundown windmill is what makes you blissfully happy and leaves you feeling that you have 'come home' then that is the only thing that matters. So long as you are happy doing it then nothing else comes into the equation. Don't let other people set the standards for *your* dream.

I think that it's important to love your work, otherwise it is very hard to make money from it; certainly this is true long-term. You have to enjoy the journey - getting rich is not about slaving over something you despise in order to make a million pounds after ten years. No amount of money can make up for doing something you hate. Plus you will lack enthusiasm and passion in your work and these are the keys to success, without these you are doomed to failure.

Do you know what your dream is? If you do then congratulations, you are very fortunate and you should go after it with all your heart. Most people have no idea what it is that they really want to do in life. Much as I would love to give you all the crucial advice that you need so that you can live a life that you love, I do not have the space here. I would need a book.

If you're struggling to find your purpose then don't allow yourself to waste another moment of your precious, irreplaceable life. Life really is too short to spend a single second of it doing something that you hate . Congratulations, you are on the first step to a happier and more fulfilling life.

Five Home Business Start-up Tips

- You can start any of these businesses today! While you must declare any extra income earned to the Inland Revenue, you can offset the proportion of domestic costs used for your business (e.g. phone, heating, lighting) against tax. The same goes for business related travel expenses. Contact your tax office for details.

- A computer and printer is a useful investment, as it can be used for writing business letters, designing and producing business stationery and adverts, maintaining accounts, storing customer/client records and dealing with mailings.

- Get some business cards printed, to give to potential customers. This helps to get your name known and presents a professional image. If you're advertising in shop windows, print cards out yourself rather than writing them by hand.

- Consider joining an agency that deals with your particular skill or profession. They'll be able to find you work and you'll retain your freelance status.

- Keep in touch with the outside world via the phone/fax/internet. Be prepared to travel in order to promote yourself and communicate with customers.

10 START UP QUESTIONS

THESE ARE THE QUESTIONS TO ASK YOURSELF
BEFORE STARTING ANY VENTURE

1.   Is there a demand for your business?

It is vital to research your market before you begin. Who is likely to buy your product or service? Where do they live? Is demand seasonal? How much will people pay for it?

2.   Have you assessed the competition?

Examine the firms in your area. Can you compete with their price, service and quality?

3.   Are there special licences or legal requirements for your business?

Contact your local authority and relevant trade organisations for advice.

4.   Do you have suitable business premises?

A desk in your own home and/or a storage space in your garage may be all you need.

5.   Do you have the right equipment?

You'll probably need a desk with a phone, and a computer and vehicle are also useful.

6. Have you contacted the tax man?

Once you move beyond selling the odd item for private sale, they will need to know what you are up to!

7. Do you have capital to put into the business?

You may need cash to buy equipment, and to cover yourself until you turn a profit. Use your own savings, ask friends and relatives, or get a cheap bank loan.

8. Have you set up a bank account?

Credit payment facilities are useful too.

9. What will your business structure be?

You could be the sole business proprietor, operate with a partner (you will need to draw up a partnership agreement) or set up a limited company. The easiest way to do this is through an accountant or company formation agency, for a small fee. You may have to hire staff too.

10. Have you produced a business plan?

It is vital to set down on paper what you are doing, with cash flow and profit projections. Not only useful for yourself, a business plan is vital when obtaining bank loans, as it shows you have done your homework.

CHAPTER 1

TURN DOODLES INTO DOSH - BECOME A FREELANCE CARTOONIST

WE ALL DREAM OF GETTING PAID FOR SOMETHING WE DO FOR FUN. Not many of us manage to achieve it though, unless we're particularly talented.

Here's an opportunity for anyone, regardless of current ability, to cash in on a well known, but much misunderstood activity: cartooning. It may not make you a fortune, but as a pleasurable, relaxing and profitable pastime it's hard to beat. If you'd like to turn your doodles into dosh, it could be just what you're looking for.

Get Noticed - With a Cartoon

Cartoons are everywhere. Books, magazines, newspapers, greeting cards, advertisements, product packaging, instruction leaflets, reports - these are just a few of the places you'll find cartoon images.

They're not all there to entertain though. Cartoon images are used to inform, educate and warn of danger as well. Research has shown time and time again that cartoon images are among the most effective attention grabbers. It's little wonder therefore that they're used so extensively.

Cartoons are so common you've probably never stopped to think who creates them or where they come from. For the most part they're created by freelancers working from home in their spare time.

Very few of these freelancers have any formal training or qualifications, because none are needed. The person deciding whether or not to buy a cartoon won't be remotely interested in qualifications or training. All they care about is the quality of the work and whether or not it does the job intended - such as make someone laugh, emphasise an informational or safety message, draw attention to an advertisement, or make a product more attractive on the shelf.

A Large, Growing Market

The market for cartoons is massive, and growing all the time. There are more magazines, newspapers and periodicals published than ever before. Hundreds are published in the UK, and there are many thousands more overseas covering every subject under the sun. They nearly all use cartoons submitted by freelancers. That's just one market ...

Advertisements, product packages and instruction booklets need attention-grabbing illustrations; business cards and letterheads need logos; T-shirts and greeting cards need designs. The list of potential markets is vast.

Start up Requirements

The great thing about cartooning is that your start up costs are close to zero and you can start in your spare time. There's no need to put anything else on hold while you give it a try. It really is an any time, any place, anywhere, opportunity.

Most people wrongly assume that artistic training is a prerequisite to getting work. Nothing could be further from the truth. In fact, people with a formal art training often have to 'unlearn' what they know in order to cartoon effectively.

Cartooning is a specialist skill which is comparatively easy to learn for the novice. The cartoon world is a very tolerant one. If you scan through a few newspapers and magazines you'll find cartoons of many styles ranging from the 'arty' to the 'rough and ready'. So there's room for cartoonists with all sorts of styles and abilities.

Getting Started

How you proceed will depend on where you're starting from. If you're already confident of your cartooning ability, the first step is to decide on the type of cartoons you'd like to draw, and from there, who is likely to be interested in buying them.

Many cartoonists specialise in one particular field. It could be anything, but one of the best places to start is publications catering for one of your interests or hobbies - something you know about. If you're a keen photographer, for example, you might want to produce some cartoons for the photographic press. In this way you'll already have a host of background knowledge to draw upon (no pun intended!).

From there, it's a case of submitting your work to the cartoon editor of the individual publication and awaiting their decision. Current NUJ (National Union of Journalists) rates for a single box cartoon are £60 to £80, rising to £400 for a colour half to full page. These are the minimum rates you should expect to be paid.

CHAPTER 2

HOW TO IMPORT OIL PAINTINGS FOR PROFIT

YOU MIGHT HAVE CONSIDERED IMPORT/EXPORT as a business opportunity before, but been a little daunted by the sheer size of it. However, here is a way that you can get started in international trade very easily indeed.

Oil paintings are a product which are very easy to deal in and very easy to import. They sell on sight, for cash, and offer an excellent profit margin too!

The secret of this business is to buy your stock from the low wage countries in the Far East. Here, talented artists are able to produce an original painting in oils on canvas for as little as £5 or so. An identical painting costs anything from £50 to £100 or more in the UK, so you can see the profit potential!

Here's how to make big money from importing oil paintings.

How to Find Suppliers

Finding suppliers takes a little time and effort, but it will be worth it at the end of the day. The best thing to do is to write to the London embassies of the various Far Eastern countries. Tell them that you are interested in importing artwork from their respective countries and you'll usually find they'll do what they can to track down suitable suppliers.

The best countries to import oil paintings from are Thailand, Malaysia, Indonesia, Taiwan, South Korea, the Philippines, India and Pakistan. Prices vary according to the source, the size and the quality, but prices start at the equivalent of £5 for basic paintings of popular subjects like flowers, street and country scenes and animals.

Once you have the addresses of suitable wholesalers, write or fax for details. They'll normally send a catalogue illustrating what subjects are available and, for a few pounds, maybe also some samples.

Some of these wholesalers also offer a very novel 'paint to order' service. All you do is mail off a photograph of your husband/wife/child/pet cat or dog, and a few weeks later they'll deliver an authentic oil painting every bit as good as if you'd paid a local artist! This can be a very useful service which offers you extra profit potential, as you'll see later.

If you are not ready to go into the import business just yet, then there are a few wholesalers around who import oil paintings and prints, allowing you to test the market before you take the plunge. Some of these are listed later. Of course, this isn't as cheap as importing direct, but it is an even easier way of getting started. At the moment one wholesaler (Art International) is advertising 5" x 7" oil paintings for £7.45 and 20" x 24" pictures for £8.95.

How to Import Oil Paintings

This is one of the easiest forms of importing you will ever find! Simply post or fax your order off to the supplier. Most of them will take a credit card in payment so you won't need to bother with bank drafts or letters of credit. Plus, depending on the card you have, you'll have some protection if your paintings don't arrive as ordered. As paintings are fairly small and light, they can be sent quite economically by air mail, so they normally only take around a week to 10 days to arrive.

The good thing about this sort of product is that you don't normally need an import licence and there are few complications with Customs. If your supplier ships with a firm like Federal Express or UPS then they will clear the goods through Customs, pay any taxes due, and then send you a bill later.

Actually, Customs duty, VAT at 17.5% on the value of the goods, plus the freight charges will mean that you are paying double the actual cost of the paintings once they reach your door. However, you'll still only be looking at a buying in cost of £10 for something that could sell for £50, £80 or even £100.

Selling Your Oil Paintings

There are so many ways of selling original oil paintings that you'll be spoilt for choice as to where to start. Perhaps the best way to start is to organise some kind of Exhibition Sale. You might have seen some of these in your own area already, and they make an ideal pastime for buyers on a Sunday afternoon or a wet bank Holiday!

Always choose a top notch location for your exhibition. You'll persuade people to pay more in a nice hotel than a draughty community centre. Also choose somewhere that is in a busy location, preferably alongside a major road. A really good place will cost you up to £300 a day, but you only need to sell two or three good paintings to get this back. Plus, when you consider that this includes all display boards, lighting and ready made passing trade, it's actually quite reasonable.

Most of your paintings should be sold unframed, as original canvasses. This makes the paintings cheaper and easier for the buyer to carry home, but the main advantage is that it allows the buyer to choose a frame which is to his/her taste rather than yours. If you wish, you can offer buyers a framing service. Simply arrange it with a local picture framing shop and add a margin on top.

The main advantage of choosing a busy location is that you won't need to do a lot of expensive press advertising. It's easy enough to make up some gaudy fluorescent hoarding and put these out on the approach roads to the hotel. Use common sense here. Put one at the entrance, one at a quarter mile, one at a half mile, and one at a mile out. This gives people time to decide to stop in for a look before they reach your venue, rather than once they're past it and then having to stop and turn round.

Other Profitable Ideas

Other methods of selling oil paintings include selling them at boot sales and Sunday markets, selling by mail order or party plan, or selling to local craft and gift shops. Some people get their paintings displayed in pubs or restaurants on a 'sale or return' basis or turn a spare room into a home art gallery.

Whatever you do, don't forget to tell people about your 'paint to order' service using photographs. Your overseas artists are unlikely to charge more than about £40 to £50 for, say, a portrait, yet you would expect to pay £200 to £300 at least for a portrait in the UK. So, you can see the profit you will make even after paying delivery charges and duties.

Once you've started importing oil paintings successfully then you might like to branch out into other items which can be sold in the same way. Handicrafts, wood carvings, jewellery, brass ware and pottery are all items which can be bought for very little in low wage countries and sold for a huge mark up here.

CHAPTER 3

CORPORATE HOSPITALITY

SETTING UP A CORPORATE HOSPITALITY BUSINESS

How to make money organising trips and entertainment for business clients

Here's an enterprise you can easily operate part time from home, earning from £500 to £20,000 - or even more - for organising just one event.

IF YOU'RE LOOKING FOR AN OPPORTUNITY that's easy to start, profitable and enjoyable, then you need to look at the corporate hospitality business. You can start off working part time from home with very little capital, yet it offers the chance to earn from £500 to £20,000 (or even more) for organising just one event!

So What Is Corporate Hospitality?

Businesses everywhere know the importance of keeping their customers happy. Corporate hospitality is simply another term for business entertaining.

The simplest kind of corporate hospitality is handing out a bottle of wine to customers at Christmas. Many bigger companies provide much more lavish hospitality than this. They

14

entertain their customers with days at the races, VIP boxes at football matches, weekends away, and even conferences and seminars in exciting and exotic places around the world.

In most cases, companies who run corporate hospitality do not do the organising themselves. They just don't have the time - or know how. Instead, they pay specialist organisers - such as you - to make all the arrangements for them. It's the ideal part time or full time opportunity if you're looking to make money and have fun too.

Success Stories: Could This Be You?

Here are just three success stories we've heard about in the world of corporate hospitality.

1.   Sam & Chris Lazzari

They formed a corporate hospitality business back in 1991. They organised events for London's merchant bankers and stockbrokers and thought nothing of hiring Concorde for their wealthy clients! Last year they sold their corporate hospitality and travel business for £2,000,000 - yes, two million pounds!

2.   Gregor Webb

He organised shooting and fishing trips in Scotland. His events are a hit with his clients, who book Gregor to entertain their American and Japanese visitors. He charges from £1,000 for a day trip, up to £5,000 or more for a weekend event.

3.   Jame Marsden

He specialises in corporate hospitality at race meets. She organises executive travel, gourmet catering and Champagne receptions for several firms in her area who use these events to entertain and impress their clients.

Easy To Start

It costs very little to set up your corporate hospitality business. You can work from home, part time. All you will need is use of a phone and, preferably, a car. By taking deposits from your clients when they order you won't necessarily need working capital.

With this type of enterprise it's vital to give a good impression. You could easily end up dealing with some very important and influential people. So, invest a little money in some good quality business note paper and business cards.

Finding Your Customers

It's not difficult to find customers for this business. Most of the companies in your area are in the market for corporate hospitality of some kind, whether it's a small event like a dinner party, or a major event like a foreign trip.

The best way to market your service is to send out a Mailshot. Write a letter telling companies about yourself and what you do. Send them to local companies in batches, until you get the response you want.

Remember, you'll find a complete, free list of all businesses in your area in your Yellow Pages. For a fee, you can even get these names and addresses on a computer disk. By loading this into just about any personal computer, you can then print out as many personalised mailshots as you need. You can also get information about local businesses at your nearest main library. In particular, ask them for membership lists of local Chambers of Commerce and Chambers of Trade.

Tip: if you can, find out the name of someone at the firm to address your letters and future correspondence to - the managing director or head of marketing will be the best person to target.

A few days after sending your mailshot, telephone each company and ask if they're interested. All you need is one or two companies to say "yes" and your new business is on its way!

Organising The Hospitality

The first step to organising corporate hospitality is to meet with your client and decide exactly what sort of event they require. Remember that the aim of the event is to promote good relations with their customers and encourage them to place more and bigger orders with a little wining and dining, or some other social event. So, the event they choose should be popular with the type of people who will be attending it. It also needs to be memorable and, if possible, distinctive or special in some way.

There's no limit to what you can organise, so just use your imagination. Below are a few ideas you could suggest.

Ten Corporate Hospitality Ideas

- **A dinner party.**

Simple but enjoyable and easy to organise. Make arrangements with a local hotel or restaurant and plan a special menu.

- **A day at the races.**

An ever popular choice. Organise transport, tickets and a buffet lunch.

- **A golfing tournament.**

Simply book time with your local course, and lay on a meal as well.

- **A sea fishing trip.**

Hire a boat and a knowledgeable local guide.

• **A day driving go-carts, rally cars, high performance cars or 4x4s.**

Contact a local race circuit and put together a package.

• **A VIP trip to a top football match.**

Organise travel, meals and book a VIP box.

• **An adventure training day/weekend**.

Have activities such as parachuting, white water rafting, canoeing and abseiling. Organise events, accommodation, equipment and insurance, etc. Ideal for adventurous clients.

• **A murder mystery weekend.**

Book a hotel and hire professional actors to act out the plot!

• **A weekend in London, Amsterdam, Paris, Monaco or New York.**

Any travel agent can organise flights and accommodation (negotiate a bulk discount). Add in airport transport, excursions and meals/activities once your clients arrive.

• **A cruise to Europe, around the Med, or even in the Caribbean.**

The latest trend in luxury corporate hospitality.

Profit Secrets: What You Need To Know

The secret of corporate hospitality is simple: don't do all the work yourself! Just do the organising and contract out as much of the actual work as possible to specialists. When it comes to charging for your services, simply charge what these suppliers charge you, and add a margin on top.

Take this typical example. You're organising a corporate hospitality trip for 12 to a top football match. You're asked to organise executive coach travel, which you arrange with a coach firm. You're asked to organise lunch en route, which you arrange with a local hotel. Finally, you contact the football club to book VIP boxes, complete with after match drinks. At the end of the day you'll have organised a fabulous corporate hospitality event for your client but not actually had to operate any of the services yourself.

Finally, simply add a margin on top of whatever the individual suppliers charge you. This is typically between 30% and 70% on top of the cost of organising an event. So, if the trip above costs £2,000 or organise, you might charge the customer a minimum of £2,600, generating a £600 profit for yourself – mostly for sitting down with your phone and organising everything!

Remember, your local Yellow Pages has most of the contacts you need. All you need to do is sit down and shop around to get the best prices. By ensuring that whoever you use is properly experienced, qualified, licensed and insured to provide that service, you can't go wrong.

Whether you want to join in the trip you've organised yourself, as the official host or hostess, is up to you – some organisers do, some don't. However, whichever way you look at it you'll have earned yourself a tidy profit from this exciting business opportunity.

CHAPTER 4

Restaurant Cabs

Every Christmas, hard hitting television advertisements press home the message that we should not drink and drive.

This is being understood by more and more people. Anyone visiting a restaurant, pub, cinema or club can be in no doubt that if they exceed the legal limit of alcohol when they are driving home, they will be punished very severely if they are caught, and there is also the possible danger to consider. The law regarding drinking and driving is something of an inconvenience to many, but you can turn it to your advantage in order to make money.

Offering a restaurant cab service is something that can not only provide a competitive and up market alternative to a normal taxi service, but will also be a big hit with restaurants and pubs. Anyone in any location with a suitable car can offer this service, providing they have the right insurance.

There are two main elements to the service. The first is similar to a taxi or chauffeur service - the driver ferries someone to the destination of their choice, be it a restaurant, pub or club, and then picks them up at an agreed time to take them home. Suitable for evening diners at local pubs and restaurants, business people at lunch time and after work, all are important potential markets.

From the point of view of the customers, the service removes the time and trouble of organising transport and they can drink as much as they want. Because it is an approved personal service, people travelling alone - particularly women - can be secure in the knowledge that they will arrive home safely and on time.

The second element actually links the service with a particular restaurant or pub (or a group/combination of them), and is the key reason why it would be popular with drinkers, diners and restaurant managers alike. It would form part of the whole restaurant meal package, with the restaurants actually advertising the cab service, and the price would be included within the cost of the meal. As a result the restaurant knows that its customers will be able to get there (and back) easily, and the single payment will be very convenient for its customers.

Therefore this service will be very attractive to restaurants and pubs, especially those situated in out of the way and rural areas. Those in particularly isolated areas are likely to benefit hugely from such a service.

To set the business up you should make sure you have a suitable saloon type car, the correct insurance, and a means of being contacted - ideally a mobile phone. Next you should contact restaurants and other licensed establishments likely to benefit from your service, negotiating either a fixed rate per customer or a commission based on the overall restaurant bill.

The advertising then becomes the responsibility of the restaurant, although you can advertise in addition, perhaps even getting your own customers. If you are working exclusively for one establishment you should charge a higher rate than you would if you were working for several. Initially at least, working for more than one might guarantee more customers.

Simple to start, with a telephone and correctly insured transport, you could launch this business within an hour. Stress the advantages of the service to restaurants and pubs and you could very soon have your own successful full or part time business.

CHAPTER 5

Advertising Portfolio Sales

Marketing can be the difference between success and failure in just about any business. The fact is that most businesses do not have the expertise to carry out effective marketing.

Consider the situation of the average small business - such as a plumbing firm. They know about installing central heating and unblocking sinks, but what do they know about creating an effective advertisement? The obvious solution is to employ a marketing consultant or advertising agency. This may be a reasonable solution for a medium sized, well established, company, but too expensive for a one man band, or company just starting out.

An opportunity exists for a service plugging the gap between the company, either cobbling something together from their own limited experience, or going to the expense of employing a consultant or advertising agency to create something original for them.

How about this example - a replacement window company. This firm could benefit from seeing the very best advertisements from competitive companies the length and breadth of the country. If the company could see these ads do you think they'd get some good advertising ideas? Do you think that the ideas that work well in one part of the country for one company, would work elsewhere for another firm?

Imagine compiling a portfolio of the very best advertisements in one field, and then selling that portfolio to all the other companies in that field. Then imagine doing the same thing in an almost infinite number of other fields!

This idea could form the basis of an excellent business, which, as far as we know, has no real competition at present. Given the scope this is an exciting opportunity. The advertising portfolios could be presented as a series of photocopies as there is little need for fancy presentation. This is essentially an information providing service.

As a starting point, you should select a number of target markets and start collecting copies of ads which relate to this field. You would be well advised to concentrate on fields where there is a high degree of advertising activity and where companies tend to work regionally rather than nationally. These fields will yield plenty of material and companies who are interested in advertising will want to know what others are doing and have the ability to pay for the information.

You could market your advertising clippings service to the companies directly, with perhaps an up front fee for all the information currently available, and then a monthly updating fee. Actual fees would depend on the field and the amount of information available. This would be a new service, so there are no rules to follow, no competitors to copy. Here is a very simple opportunity with almost limitless potential. There is little to lose by giving it a try.

CHAPTER
6

City Dog Park

Any dog owner who lives in a busy town or city will know how difficult it is to give their dog the exercise they require. Dogs are already forbidden from most shops and many shopping centres. Parks may be few and far between and there are hefty fines for dog fouling.

All this is likely to make pooch and his owner feel rather unwanted. However, there is a business idea that can give our four legged friends the freedom they need and help us make money in the process.

The dog park, a successful American idea, in a city area - usually the roof of a tower block or skyscraper - given over to dogs. The park has enough space to let dogs run free and get as much exercise as they require, while still having places where the dogs can sleep, eat and be fenced off from one another, if necessary. The whole area is self contained so that the dogs cannot escape.

Dog owners can leave their treasured pets with an attendant at the park before heading off to work or to do their shopping. They would either pay a daily/hourly/weekly fee, or pay in advance on a membership basis. The attendant then ensures that the dog is fed, watered, exercised, on or off the lead, and generally takes care of the dog's well being. At the end of the day, the dogs are collected by their owners and the whole area is cleaned up.

There is scope for expanding the service so that owners can leave their dogs for days and weeks at a time. The parks would have an advantage over traditional dog kennels as they would be nearby and offer the dogs plenty of exercise. Other tie-in services you could provide are dog grooming and cleaning, and veterinary visits. The dog park could also have a shop selling food and everything else a dog might require.

To set up the service you will first need to rent a suitable space. Roofs of buildings are ideal, as they are self contained, offer sufficient space, can be easily leased at relatively low cost, and have all the necessary amenities nearby. You will need to ensure that there is suitable access by lift or stairs. There may be suitable areas on ground level, although land of this type tends to be more expensive to rent and fence off, or is too far away from people's houses and places of work.

The type of person who would require this service is likely to be fairly affluent so you can charge highly for it. Advertise in pet shops, veterinary surgeries and in the local press. Also have some business cards made which can be left in the canteens and reception areas of local businesses and handed out as necessary.

Although this business may require an initial investment, - for rent, fencing, food and cleaning equipment - it is something that anyone with a love of dogs will be able to do with the minimum of help and does not require any previous experience or qualifications. Very successful in towns and cities across the US, the idea is just begging to be tried here!

CHAPTER 7

Home Security Service

How many of us go on holiday with the dreaded thought in the back of our minds that while we are away our homes could fall prey to burglars or vandals, or else be affected by some kind of natural disaster such as fire or burst pipes?

For many people, just thinking of these possibilities can effectively ruin a holiday, but there is a service you can offer which will banish these thoughts from people's minds and help you make some money too. The business which can do this is the home security service, and is an excellent opportunity for anyone who has transport and a little time on their hands. By providing this service you can offer peace of mind for anyone leaving their homes unattended. The home security guard checks up on each client's house while they are away, making sure that milk, newspapers and letters are all cleared away from the doorstep, checking that all doors and windows are kept secure, and generally ensuring that the house is maintained and does not look empty. There may be additional requirements to water plants, feed pets, tidy up inside, air rooms, and more.

One reason why this business can be so profitable is that it is not confined to looking after people's homes when they are on holiday. It can also include taking care of people's second homes.

Since the property boom of the mid 1980s, a huge number of second homes have been bought in the UK, either as an investment or as a place to escape to during the Summer Holidays, Weekends, and Bank Holidays. Places like Devon, Cornwall, Wales and East Anglia are well known as areas that are full of holiday homes. They do not just exist in the seaside and traditional holiday areas, but in the countryside surrounding any major town or city, there will be cottages, houses and flats that provide a weekend escape for people spending their working week in the city.

As they are generally visited only at weekends or on certain weeks of the year, these properties will be unoccupied for at least 80 per cent of the time. As a result they could fall prey to thieves and vandals and are often prone to potential damage from wind and rain, fire and burst pipes. Since the owners are not always on hand to check up on their property, it makes sense to have someone on call who can.

The home security guard calls on each property perhaps daily or twice a week, or whatever frequency the client requires, making an examination of the property and premises.

There is ample scope for developing the service to suit customers' budgets and needs. As well as the basic duties, you could offer a more regular and/or thorough service for people willing to pay more. Perhaps checking all doors, windows, gates and outhouses, and even going as far as to make a full internal and external inspection.

The service can be expanded to include basic upkeep of the property, perhaps including watering plants, cleaning windows, airing rooms, mowing lawns and doing the gardening. You could also deal with any repairs and improvements that need to be carried out, either doing these yourself if you have the experience, or subcontracting them to local handymen, plumbers, electricians, gardeners and so on. Another duty could be preparing the house for when the owners visit or when the holidaymakers return, so that they get milk, newspapers, hot water and flowers in the rooms when they arrive.

Charges could begin at £15 per basic visit, ranging to £50 or more per week for a more comprehensive service. In fact, depending on the level of service you offer (and the size of your client's wallet!) you could charge a great deal more than this. Also, you could charge more during holiday periods in the same way that holiday companies charge more, to take account of the increased demand.

One place to advertise is in the property section of local newspapers, although the best way to get customers is through word of mouth. Talk to the local shopkeepers, vendors, publicans and other homeowners about your service. Perhaps placing ads in local shops, pubs, and so on and encourage any clients to recommend your service to others. Once you get your first few customers, your reputation for vigilance, efficiency, discretion and friendliness, will spread and your business will grow.

With the property market on the up again, the second home security business would appear to be increasingly secure. People are always conscious of the possible damage to their homes from crime and natural causes when they go on holiday. Since people will pay for peace of mind, you should find that the home security business will be a profitable one.

CHAPTER 8

Cleaning Extractor Fans and Gutters
Why cleaning extractor fans and gutters can be a glamorous business (true!).

The idea of making a living from cleaning gutters and extractor fans may not sound particularly glamorous.

As a result there is a big untapped demand for this service, and those that do provide it make the kind of money that can easily pay for three weeks in the Caribbean every year. Does it sound a little more glamorous now? The old saying "Where there's muck, there's money" is certainly true today.

A business as a cleaner of gutters and extractor fans can be started up for next to nothing. All you need is a ladder, transport and some cloths, brushes and occasionally a few basic tools. You do not need any special experience or licences.

So how do you start up this business?

There are likely to be some council owned estates in your area - perhaps you live in one. Pick any street, perhaps the street you live in, and check the condition of the guttering. It is unlikely it will have been cleaned in many years and it may be in a poor state of repair. Estimate the number of hours it would take you to clean the whole street's gutters, multiply this by your hourly rate - about £10 per hour is not unreasonable to begin with - add to this the cost of mending or replacing any broken guttering. Congratulations, you have just put together your first job estimate!

You should then take your estimate to your local council engineer. Offer to clean/fix the street's guttering for this price. What you should find is that they jump at your offer, as councils tend to find it very difficult to get contractors to do such a small job. You can then find out what other streets need doing and the work should escalate from there.

If the council engineer turns down your offer, don't worry. It may just be a case of looking for the right street or the right time to clean it, or dropping your price a little. There is also the option of cleaning the gutters of privately owned houses. Few people want to clear their gutters out - believe it! Simply drop your cost estimate through letterboxes together with your address and phone number.

Once people realise how cheap and quick the service is, and how blocked and broken guttering can damage the rest of the property, they will most likely pay for a clean. Once you have cleaned a client's guttering, <u>make an appointment to come back in six months or a year to do it again</u>. An extra service you could offer is to install wire mesh that prevents leaves from clogging up the guttering. Whilst up the ladder, check for loose, broken or missing tiles. Then link up with a local roofer and claim 15% of his invoice as a commission.

Of course, this is only half of the picture. Take a look at the extractor fans used in the businesses, shops, factories, schools, offices, pubs, restaurants, leisure centres, and so on in your area. Chances are they'll be extremely dirty, and probably won't have been cleaned in years.

Your next step is to point out to the businesses concerned that their extractor fans, by being dirty and partially blocked, are not functioning as energy efficiently as they should be and are also representing a potential threat to health and safety. Send them your quote for cleaning the fan perhaps following this up with a phone call.

Again, you should find that if your price is right, you will pick up plenty of trade. <u>Don't forget to make a future cleaning appointment after each job</u>. Any city of moderate size should have enough fans to keep you in business, and once you become more familiar with them, you could do repairs or even contact the fans' manufacturers offering to be their official maintenance engineer.

Overall, cleaning gutters and extractor fans represents an extremely viable, low cost, business that could earn a substantial amount of money.

CHAPTER 9

GROUND FORCE

SET UP YOUR OWN GARDENING BUSINESS

Gardening can be both a relaxing pastime and a profitable, low cost, easy to start business. Here is our guide to setting up your own cutting (h)edge gardening enterprise

` GARDENS ARE PLACES WHERE WE CAN TAKE A WELCOME BREAK from our hectic lifestyles and noisy, polluted cities. Many home and business owners just do not have the time or inclination to maintain them.

This presents the perfect opportunity to establish a profitable home gardening business. The initial costs are small and if you are lucky you may get to ride around in the sun on a motorised lawnmower.

Gardening Business Basics

You don't need to be particularly green fingered to start a simple gardening maintenance service. Although it does involve a certain amount of strenuous effort, it requires no prior experience and start up costs can be minimal.

Many one man (and woman) gardeners work solely for private householders. These clients fall into two camps: those with plenty of money but little time or willingness to do gardening jobs, and elderly people who enjoy their garden but who are no longer physically able to do the work themselves. By doing a good job and developing a good relationship with clients you can soon generate enough work to put you in profit and keep you busy.

There is also big money to be made working for corporate clients. Many large offices, for example, have extensive grounds which need to be maintained. Since the demise of council parks departments many gardeners have profited by taking on a team of casual staff and tendering for local authority contracts.

Bear in mind that this is a seasonal business and you will have to work extra hard in summer to get you through the lean times in winter. You will also need to be prepared for anything the British weather can throw at you. For most, however, the easy going working conditions, friendly client relationships and odd spells of fine weather make this the business to be in.

Training and Qualifications

You don't need any formal qualifications to become a gardener, but if you can provide any you'll stand a better chance of impressing potential clients. Your local further education college will advise you on NVQ, HND, BTEC and degrees.

Aside from formal qualifications, the best training you can have is experience. Offer to work in garden centres at weekends and read as much as possible about the main subject areas.

Also remember that you're operating a business. You'll need to understand how to keep your finances in order, particularly if the tax man should pay a visit. Update your accounts regularly and always keep your receipts. It may be worth investing in a part time business management course.

Good fitness and stamina is vital, as the work is extremely physical. You also need good people skills - word of mouth recommendations are important, so you must concentrate on building up a good relationship with your clients.

What Kind of Gardening Business?

Before you begin, you will need to decide on the direction of your business. Gardening can be divided into three main categories.

• **Maintenance** - The best option for anyone starting out. The work is mainly physical and you will require only a basic understanding of plants. You will be expected to keep clients' gardens in order, involving tasks such as mowing the lawn, watering plants, weeding, pruning hedges and trees, and clearing leaves. Your client will usually tell you what needs doing, and will say whether they want you to come back on a regular basis. It is useful to be able to offer general advice and tips, although you can find such information in any gardening reference book. The going rate for maintenance varies from around £5 up to £20 per hour depending on the client, the area, and the duties involved.

• **Landscaping and Design** -This involves designing and building garden features such as paths, rockeries, flower beds, ponds and other water features. It is more profitable than maintenance, but still involves a certain amount of labour. Designers plan which flowers go where, to create an impressive display of floral delights. So alongside your knowledge of plants, soil types and so on, you will need good creative judgement and an ability to interpret the owner's requirements.

• **Consultancy** - This is for someone who really knows their stuff. Consultants will be expected to advise on a wide range of gardening topics, from organic fertilisers and pruning tips to climatic growth rates. Corporate clients may want advice on what indoor plants and shrubs will best suit their premises. If you are also able to supply the necessary items this can be fantastically lucrative, and this need not involve any physical work at all.

You will know which of these areas best suits your knowledge, ability and interests. This article concentrates on starting a basic gardening maintenance business, which for most is the natural place to start, at least until you begin to develop an understanding of horticulture, landscaping and design.

Buying Your Equipment

Although some clients will have their own garden tools which you can use, you should carry your own set of essentials such as gloves, clippers, a trowel, spade, fork, and preferably a watering can, lawn mower and wheelbarrow. By shopping around and buying second-hand maybe from factory shops, the basic tools could be purchased for a total of under £100.

Be realistic when buying equipment. You can impress clients with a new £3,000 ride on rotary mower with petrol engine, but how many gardens will be big enough to accommodate it? Start with the basics and gather more items as your earnings increase. Consider quality as well as price - a cheap fork may rust away in six months, whereas an expensive one could last a lifetime.

Occasionally, you will need expensive gear such as a rotavator, chipper, chain saw or sit down mower. It is best to hire these as and when you need them, rather than paying for them outright.

Another important consideration is transport. Ideally you should have a van or truck for carrying tools and ferrying old branches and twigs to the dump. A small transit van will cost around £12,000 new, with annual insurance costs of about £300.

Initially it may be possible to do without if you are working for clients who already own the basic tools.

Finally, it is worth investing in either a mobile phone or answering machine so you can take bookings from clients when you are out on a job.

Promoting Your Business

Once you've purchased your equipment it is time to look for business. Concentrate your marketing to cover, say, a 25 mile radius around where you live. Garden maintenance services tend to use the following means of promotion.

- Personal recommendations through friends and family.
- Postcards placed in shop windows, post offices, libraries, supermarket notice boards, etc.
- Personal calls to householders (this works best in well off neighbourhoods - look for large and/or poorly maintained gardens.

Each of these marketing methods is cheap and effective, but it can take a while to build a solid client base. To speed things up you may wish to get a Yellow Pages listing and place classified ads in the local paper. Another effective tactic is to distribute flyers at garden centres and through letter boxes.

When you find a new client, work hard at impressing them so that they decide to employ you on a regular basis. As an incentive you could offer them a (cheaply purchased) free plant of some variety. Give satisfied clients a few of your flyers or business cards to hand to friends.

You should aim for the affluent premises, as employing a gardener is generally considered something of a luxury. You need not focus solely on private homeowners - many businesses have gardens or plots of land that need tending and developing. By adding companies to your customer list you could find yourself with a regular source of income should your private work decline.

Be prepared to spend at least £100 on advertising and marketing to get your business off the ground. Remember, you won't be the only gardener in the area - your competition may be well established and you will need to get people's attention. Starting a gardening business is no bed of roses.

Legal Aspects

As environmental legislation becomes increasingly intrusive and tough, you will be expected to comply with all such measures. Chemical pesticides and fertilisers, together with most other chemically based agents, often have restricted usage. If you introduce any poisonous plants into a garden be sure to inform the owner, especially if they have pets and children.

Make sure you have a sound understanding of The Control of Substances Hazardous to Health Regulations and The Control of Pesticides Act. The 1959 Weeds Act will inform you of poisonous weeds and the regulations governing them, and you should also be aware of the Wildlife and Country Act of 1981. This Act covers endangered plants which should be left alone. Finally, the Health and Safety at Work Act should be strictly observed, particularly if you intend to employ others who might operate machinery .

If you are concerned at the damage chemical based pesticides and fertilisers cause, why not operate on a strictly organic level? This could be a great marketing device, as many people these days are rightly concerned at the environmental damage they may unwittingly be causing. You could encourage a whole new generation of environmentally concerned homeowners to employ you as a result of your conscientious policies. (Make sure you remember not to use peat extracted from protected marshland, as this may cause bad publicity.)

Branching Out

If you succeed as a general gardener you may, after a few years, wish to specialise in certain areas, or even start up your own nursery. Designing, landscaping and consultancy are profitable avenues to explore. Expert gardeners are always needed, not only by homeowners but by garden centres and businesses too.

By the time you begin to consider specialising you'll already have built up quite a reputation, at least in your local area. By attending important horticultural events and displaying your own achievements you will get your name recognised by the people who matter.

Useful Contacts

The following organisations can provide advice and guidance when setting up a gardening business.

* **British Association of Landscape Industries,** *Landscape House, 9 Henry Street, Keighley, West Yorkshire BD21 3DR*
Tel: 01535 606139
* **Commercial Horticulture Association,** *Links View House, 8 Fulwith Avenue, Harrogate, North Yorkshire HG2 8HR*
Tel: 01423 879208
* **Garden Trade News** - *Tel: 01733 898100*
* **Grower Magazine** - *Tel: 01322 660070*
* **Society of Garden Designers,** *6 Borough Road, Kingston upon Thames, Surrey KT2 6BD*
Tel: 020 8974 9483
* **The Good Gardeners Association,** *Pinetum, Churcham, Gloucester G12 8AD*
Tel: 01452 750 402.

CHAPTER 10

PROFITABLE PUBLICATIONS
START YOUR OWN NEWSLETTER

Our guide to creating your own mega money magazine or newsletter explains how to market and sell your publications.

FROM THE CHEAPEST photocopied fanzine to the glossy monthlies such as Loaded or Cosmopolitan, publishing can be a highly lucrative business.

It is a fantastic way to make money from your own talents and interests. It is possible to earn a substantial income from creating and selling your own publication and - like Viz for instance - a modest kitchen table enterprise can become a huge success.

Study the basics of setting up a magazine. Decide on the content, size, means of production, and so on, and put it all together. We explain how to market your publication and turn it into a mega money success.

How Much Should You Charge?

Once you have finalised what your magazine will look like and how it is to be produced, you must decide how much to charge for it. There are two major factors to consider: costs, and market forces.

Only you can calculate your costs. Examine and list all outgoings, including author payments, stationery, printing, advertising, and overheads. When you have added them all together you can arrive at a rough idea of how much each copy of your magazine will cost to produce. This is the minimum you can charge to break even.

You then need to examine the market place. Charge too much and readers won't bite because they won't see value for money. Charge too little and you won't cover your costs.

So consider your target audience. Do they have money? You may be able to sell a glossy magazine costing £5 to the owner of a big house in the posh end of town, but would a penniless student buy it? Identify your potential readers to assess what they are willing and able to pay.

A sound tactic is to examine your nearest rivals to see what they charge. Then decide what your target audience might be willing to spend on your publication.

Marketing and Promotion

Now to the toughest part of the overall task - selling your publication. If you've researched your subject properly you will have pinpointed the target readership. This is essential - no successful magazine got where it did without knowing its audience intimately.

If you know your potential readers you will know their spending habits, what periodicals they read and the establishments they frequent. This information will influence how and where you choose to advertise your magazine and sell it.

You could, for instance, place advertisements or flyers in other publications, which can be a useful platform for publicising your own. You could also send review copies of your launch issue to interested magazines for review purposes. A good review is at least as good as a display advertisement.

Don't overlook your local newspaper or freesheet. They are always on the lookout for interesting copy on local achievers, and a quick phone call to the news desk is usually all it takes to get someone interested in reviewing your newsletter, or writing an article about it. Whenever you discuss your project, keep plugging the title of your magazine and saying where it is available.

Another way to get your magazine known is to send out a sales letter and/or other promotional materials by post to likely customers. A tried and tested method is to buy a mailing list from a specialist list broker who knows the business.

Make sure the names and addresses they supply are those of people who will be genuinely interested in your publication (for example, for a fishing magazine you might buy a list that contains subscribers to other fishing magazines, and/or the names and addresses of recent buyers of equipment from fishing shops). Also ensure that the list you buy has been updated recently, and not so long ago that the people have lost interest in your subject, moved to another address, or died.

You can find list brokers in your local Yellow Pages under the heading Direct Mail. Ring a few for details on their price lists and analyse just what they have to offer, including guarantees on age, frequency of updates, and whether the names listed are from enquirers or buyers - buyers' names are better than enquirers but are more expensive.

Some important points: even with top quality mailing lists the response rate won't be above 5%. You may get no response at all if your promotional materials are not up to scratch, or if you mail to too few customers. So, while you can get excellent returns from this method of advertising, you must do your sums carefully in order to ensure your mailshot will be cost effective.

No matter what form your marketing takes, your promotional materials need to hit just the right spot. This could be the subject of a full article in its own right, but basically you must outline all the benefits the reader will gain by subscribing to your publication. If you get your message right, the result will be a flood of subscription cheques.

Advertising Revenue

One source of revenue never to be overlooked is advertising. By selling space to businesses related to the subject of your magazine you can make a considerable income over and above your subscription sales. (Indeed, some publications survive on it. Some city based free newspapers contain advertising which comprises over three quarters of the total copy. This fact, coupled with a circulation as high as 80,000 copies, ensures a hefty profit.)

Clearly, a one person newsletter operated from home can't compete with bigger publications. But even so, the additional income from advertising can mean the different between the survival and failure and so should never be dismissed as a potential source of revenue.

Your New Publication: KEY POINTS

• **Analyse the competition - ensure your publication offers something different.**
• **Settle on the ideal level and style of material.**
• **Select the right look and length for your magazine or newsletter, taking into account overall costs and demand.**
• **Choose the most cost effective printing process.**
• **Decide what tasks you can do yourself and what tasks to contract out.**

- **Price your product according to what your target audience might be willing to spend.**
- **Devise your marketing strategy.**
- **Consider selling advertising space as an additional source of income.**

Getting Your Sums Right

Before you launch into your venture, ensure your financial calculations are right. Consider all the costs involved and work out the various profit permutations depending on how well your publication sells.

Also bear in mind your time commitment. If you decide to do everything yourself, consider the hours you (and your assistants, if any) will need to spend on each process: writing, editing, typesetting, pasting up and scanning, checking, printing, collating, folding, stapling, guillotining, addressing, envelope stuffing, marketing, and record keeping.

Overall, remember that if you get everything right and can tap into a vein of interested readers you can generate a profitable - and hugely enjoyable - business. Perhaps your publication can capture the public's imagination and cash in the way that Chris Donald's Viz has done.

Useful Information

The following contains useful information on publications currently available. Each is updated and published annually. Your library should have at least one of these publications. Alternatively, you can order them from good book shops, or obtain them direct from the publisher, whose addresses are provided.

The Writers Handbook: Macmillan General Books, 25 Eccleston Place, London W1W 9NF.
Writers and Artists Yearbook: A & C Black (Publishers) Ltd., 35 Bedford Row, London WC1R 4JH.

Willings Press Guide: *(published in two volumes - one UK and one overseas); Reed Information Services, Windsor Court, East Grinstead House, East Grinstead, West Sussex RH19 1XA.*

Small Press Guide: *Writers Book shop, 7-11 Kensington High Street, London W8 5NP.*

Lights List: *Photon Press, 29 Longfield Road, Tring, Herts HP23 4DG.*

A Guide to British Mail Order Magazines and Adsheets: *John Pooley, 27 Carey Street, Reading RG1 7JS.*

The International Directory of Little Magazines and Small Presses: *Dustbooks, PO Box 100, Paradise, CA 95967, USA. (Details can be obtained from the American publisher in exchange for an International Reply Coupon, obtainable from your Post Office.)*

CHAPTER 11

DIAL A PROFIT
LOCAL SERVICE PHONE BOOKS

THE LOCAL SERVICE PHONE BOOK is an excellent easy start money maker. It can be started without prior experience in any town or city, and will generate a substantial ongoing income. Here's how it works.

When you have a household emergency – a burst pipe, say – what usually happens? After searching for the phone book you discover there are three or four pages of listings for plumbers. Who do you call?

If you are lucky, you or a friend will already know a reputable firm. What if, as is usually the case, you don't?

You could work your way through the list and get quotes from each plumber, but it is an emergency and you need someone quickly. In this situation people generally end up going for the nearest firm, or the one with the biggest ad. The problem with this is that you have no idea how reliable the firm is, or whether their charges are reasonable. This is a difficulty that most people face. So why not help them and make money at the same time – with the local service phone book.

The concept is simple. You publish an 'at a glance' directory containing the important numbers people need in an emergency, and for general everyday use. The idea is that people will keep it handy, perhaps even pin it up next to their telephone. Your earnings come from charging firms to participate.

Getting Firms to Participate

The first step is to contact a range of local services, covering anything from emergency household services to restaurants, explaining that you are publishing a one page directory which will be distributed to everyone in town. You earn money by getting the firms to pay a fee to be your 'Approved Local Supplier', of which there is one per category. Extra money can be made by charging them to have an additional ad printed on the back of the directory.

So the firm gets extra coverage and an advantage over its competitors. People at home get a list of useful services that have been vetted and approved, with just one number to ring. You get to make a hefty profit!

Why Are Freephone Numbers Used?

To give the concept a unique selling point it is best to make the guide an 0800 freephone directory. Under each heading you list the firm's 0800 number (e.g. Plumber: 0800 XXXXX) which puts the customer straight through to an approved firm free of charge. If people know the numbers are free they are more likely to use the directory, and the firms get more responses as a result.

Searching for potential advertisers is a simple process. Make a list of categories covering household services (e.g. plumber, electrician), home improvements (e.g. builder, glazier), everyday use (e.g. taxi, pizza delivery or take away), motoring (e.g. car hire, garage) and professional and financial services (e.g. solicitor, loan company).

You can probably fit around 50 categories into your directory. When you have a list of categories, take your Yellow Pages or Thomson Directory and, for each category, contact firms (preferably those who already have a freephone number) explaining your business. Emphasise that a listing may generate many thousands of responses locally. Aim to get one firm per category, and sell as much additional advertising space as you can.

Substantial Potential Revenue

Of course, the hard part is convincing people to advertise, so you will need a friendly and persuasive manner. Just look at the potential revenue for a guide you print and update every year. By publishing a directory in a number of localities you can develop a lucrative full time business Once established, you have the potential to be making £30,000 plus a year – by helping people out in an emergency!

CHAPTER 12

ADVERTISING ON THE MOVE GETTING NOTICED WITH MOBILE ADS

Established methods of getting yourself and your business noticed generally require a lot of time, effort and expense to work. Here is an outline of an alternative form of advertising that is not only a superb form of promotion, but can also form the basis of a business.

A few months ago a friend and I decided to try out a new hotel restaurant we had heard about. On arrival we were most impressed with the opulent surroundings, and millions had clearly been spent on this previously neglected Grade II listed building.

We were seated in a fabulous dining room. A pianist played melodically in the back ground and the food was excellent. Only one thing marred the evening: the atmosphere. We were the only diners in the entire place! We couldn't understand it, as the surroundings were perfect, the food was fine, the service was friendly and efficient. Even the prices were reasonable. We were baffled.

When I spoke to others about my experience, it emerged that hardly anyone knew about the restaurant's existence. It seemed incredible that so much money was poured into the venture and so little was used to advertise its opening.

Cheap to run - a mobile advertising service will cut through the apathy

Well, you can't keep a good thing down for long, and despite a faltering start, the hotel and restaurant have thrived. It seems a pity that the marketing of the business was handled so badly. It doesn't matter how good your business or service is if people do not know about you.

One of the difficulties with regular mainstream advertising is that we, the public, switch off. We are bombarded with TV ads, radio ads, newspapers and leaflets - even our cars are targeted when we leave them in a car park.

Here's a novel way of advertising that cuts through the apathy. You simply can't ignore it. It's a great business start up opportunity. Alternatively, it may just be what you need to promote your own business. Either way, we think you will be interested.

The Concept

Mobile advertising in this country is still very much in its infancy. All you need to stand out from the crowd is a converted vehicle which will carry advertising hoarding. The beauty of the idea is that it is so flexible. The poster van can either park up in a busy location, or be driven along a prearranged route depending on the client's requirements. A combination of the two methods is usually most effective.

Getting Started

The Vehicle

This will be your most expensive outlay. You will need a vehicle that is no bigger than a transit van, and ideally it should fit a parking meter space. The hoarding should comprise waterproof posters, which can be mounted on a double sided triangular plywood construction, fitting onto both sides of the van with its apex above the roof.

The Posters

A pair of posters on either side of the vehicle will ensure the client's message gets maximum exposure. There are various ways in which this can be done. One is to hand paint messages onto a wipe clean surface. This is best done by a professional sign writer. When done properly it cannot be distinguished from print. Alternatively, you could use a computer desktop publishing package. Some computer printers are able to handle large posters, although you could tile up A4 sized sheets to create a large display. If you are unsure how to proceed, contact several printers and/or designers (see your Yellow Pages) who will fill you in on what is available. Remember, whichever method you choose, it must be able to withstand the elements.

The Drivers

Enlist the services of a couple of part time drivers. This will ensure you have a back up if someone is ill or on holiday.

Promoting the Business

This couldn't be easier. Simply use your poster van, when not booked out to clients, to promote your service. For example, your message could say, "Hire This Vehicle" in large letters, along with a short list of promotional uses and a contact telephone number.

Pricing the Service

Prices can be worked out on a daily, weekly or monthly rate depending on the client's needs. Perhaps the simplest way to price the service is to work out the cost of the artwork, design and sign writing, which will be a one off fee. Use this as a basis for deciding your daily rate, which should obviously cover your total costs, plus a profit mark up. Check out other forms of advertising in your area and remember to cost in your driver's time and vehicle expenses before fixing a price.

Assuring the Client

Advertising costs are always difficult to justify. Clients may feel worried about getting value for money. You can dispel their anxiety in several ways.

There's nothing like personal recommendation, so save letters from satisfied customers to show the client. Or, provide them with one or two customer phone numbers so they can speak to them directly. Obviously you will need to ask their permission beforehand.

Guarantee that the poster van will be visible for ten hours daily.

At the end of the campaign give the client a full report of prime sites visited. Back this up with photographic evidence.

Additional Services

All kinds of complementary services can be incorporated into the advertising package. For example, if you were asked to promote a fair you could use balloons or employ clowns, stilt walkers or cheer leaders in the same area as the mobile poster van to really draw the crowds. The only limit is the client's budget.

Adapting the Business to Suit

This business can be run from suitable premises, or from home if space allows. If start up capital is a problem, you could adapt the concept to suit your pocket. You could use the roof rack on your own vehicle to create a scaled down version of the idea. If demand allows, there is no reason why you can't add another vehicle or two to keep pace with demand.

While the advertising market is extremely competitive, mobile ads are a fantastic way to get your business **_really_** moving.

CHAPTER 13

TURN £50 TO £500 IN FIVE DAYS!

DO YOU WANT TO MAKE MONEY FAST?

Here is an excellent project which you can start immediately with little investment and get a return on it very quickly.

This project is based on actual businesses operating today, so with a little effort you too could start making money straight away.

Earn ten times your initial investment in just five days!

Leafleting Service

Distributing leaflets door to door is, pound for pound, cheaper than TV, radio or newspaper advertising. Small businesses are likely to benefit from a leafleting service, as they will rarely have time to organise one themselves, so market your services to local shops, restaurants, garages, tradesmen, or anyone who might require the service.

Try to see the business manager or owner, offering to deliver leaflets to, for example, 5,000 homes for a fixed rate per thousand. It is useful to know your dropping area beforehand, perhaps tailoring your drop to deliver only to certain houses or areas, or saving time by distributing leaflets at large housing estates or blocks of flats.

It is reasonable to expect that around a quarter of businesses will be interested in the service. The key is to build up the number of clients so that you can deliver many leaflets at a time, decreasing time and effort expended and increasing income.

Pick up your leaflets to distribute from the customer prior to the drop. Usually the customer organises the design and print, but if you have the capability, then offer to do it for them, charging extra for the service. An advantage is that you will not have to invest anything until you find your customers.

Over the five day period you could easily deliver between 5,000 to 8,000 leaflets, perhaps working on evenings and weekends if preferred. Expenses are likely to be around £35 for travel and £15 for telephone calls. If you delivered 6875 leaflets for a total of four customers at one time, at a cost of £20 per thousand, then you will have profits of £500.

CHAPTER 14

HOW TO SAVE - AND MAKE - MONEY
BUYING REPOSSESSED AND
BANKRUPT GOODS

Here's the insider's guide to government auctions.
Discover how easy it is to buy repossessed items
and bankrupt stock for next to nothing.

NO, A GOVERNMENT AUCTION DOESN'T involve selling off cabinet ministers to theme parks and museums (you wish!). It is simply a collective term for any auction arranged by a government department, such as Customs and Excise, the Tax Department, and council bailiffs.

The main thing you need to know is that government auctions are a source of amazing BARGAINS. The stock generally comes from deceased estates, repossessions and bankrupt businesses. Auctions are the easiest way to recoup some cash in the shortest possible time, but the emphasis is on selling the goods quickly rather than getting a good price. So anyone who attends the auction can walk away with quality goods for next to nothing.

Ignore the popular preconception that auctions are just for antique dealers and art traders. Whether you're after a quality second-hand vehicle or a lap top computer, the chances are you'll find whatever you're searching for in one of the many lots that will go under the hammer. Similarly, no matter what you've seen on TV, it takes more than a facial twitch to secure a product at auction, so don't fret about accidentally bidding your house away while trying to contain a sneeze.

While it is best to attend a couple of auctions first in order to understand what's going on, the viewing and bidding process is actually very simple.

What Can You Buy?

You'll find all manner of products, ranging from electrical goods to sofas and dining furniture, usually at unbelievably low prices. Let's look at a few examples.

◆ **Antiques / Furniture**

Fancy a set of three Victorian chairs for £10, or an antique solid oak dresser for £130? They could easily be yours at auction. Whether you want to fill your house with antique furniture or simply something that looks nice, you can do it for around 10% of the high street retail price by getting them from a government auction.

◆ **Cycles**

If you're the type of person who enjoys hurtling down 90 degree embankments at breakneck speeds, you could pick up a fantastic mountain bike for next to nothing. A top of the range Peugeot cycle, unclaimed after being recovered by police, was recently sold for just £15.

◆ **Cars**

For a slightly more luxurious ride, how about a saving of £8,500 on a Jaguar XJS? The vehicle had been confiscated by HM Customs and Excise and was in near showroom condition.

✦   Computers
An IBM Pentium 4 PC was recently sold for a staggering £95 - that's a machine that retails for over £800!

✦   Office Goods
An answering machine bought for £5 and a photocopier for £20, sold at an auction of bankrupt business stock, could help you get a business off the ground cheaply, or you could sell them on.

✦   Kitchen Equipment
Whether you want a virtually new washing machine for £30 or a fridge for £5 requiring minor repairs, auctions are a great place for bargains.

✦   Other Items
Other stock commonly sold off cheaply at auction includes TV, video, Hi-fi gear, musical instruments, power tools, and all manner of ex-business stock and equipment.

The reason such large savings can be made is both simple and completely legitimate. Every year, thousands of businesses go bankrupt. For those involved it is an ugly experience, but for everyone else it can be a godsend. Computers, fax machines, printers, and all manner of office equipment, are sold off at auction to pay off company debts.

The same applies to stolen vehicles, bicycles, jewellery and any other stolen goods seized by police, which are also sold off at government auctions. You'll be aware of the high crime rate in the UK, so you can imagine the huge reserves of goods that build up in government and police storage rooms over a relatively short period of time. As it is illegal for the bodies in possession to simply sell the items to friends and family, government auctions are arranged with the sole intention of getting rid of these huge stockpiles.

Where To Find Government Auctions

Government auctions are rarely advertised, which is why most people don't know they exist. You can find them by contacting local auction houses - simply look in your Yellow Pages or similar under Auctioneers. Contact the firms asking if they handle sales of government stock. if they do, ask to be put on their mailing list. That way you'll get at least one month's notice of any forthcoming events. You should also receive a catalogue so you can identify any lots that particularly interest you.

If you have difficulty in locating an auction nearby, dates and locations can be obtained from the sources listed at the end of this article. Both Government Auction News and The Auctioneer newsletters list locations and schedules of auctions across the UK. Another possibility is to contact your local Official Receiver and enquire as to the whereabouts of their regular auction houses (alternatively, try phoning the Insolvency Service or the Department of Trade and Industry - the phone numbers are listed at the end of this article.

Persevere in your detective work. For the sake of a couple of phone calls you could save yourself hundreds, even thousands, of pounds. Don't give up if you find yourself travelling a considerable distance to attend an auction - the rewards will far outweigh the travelling costs.

What To Do When You Get There

You've read about the fantastic bargains on offer. You've located a government auction, and you've travelled a couple of hundred miles to attend it. So what now?

Well, if you've got any sense you'll put your money away, get a coffee and take some time to observe the events around you. The last thing you want to do is jump in at the deep end and start buying everything in sight. You'll be surrounded by professional traders, most of whom will be able to spot a bargain at a hundred paces. Watch them and see which goods they take interest in.

Many auctions have pre-sale days when potential bidders can peruse the lots to assess the quality of products up for sale. It's a good idea to attend them. Few professionals would consider buying a second-hand car, for instance, without first assuring its quality, so why should you be any different?

By spending time at different auctions before you begin to actively participate you'll learn some of the tricks of the trade. For example, you may find a product displaying an "as seen" label. This should make you suspicious - auctioneers aren't required to specify individual problems and the "as seen" label indicates the likely presence of some kind of fault or damage.

Don't expect much in terms of warranties - more and more auctions are refusing to offer them. However, the savings you stand to make far outweigh the overall risks. Chances are, that photocopier which cost £20 will be in perfect working order, saving you hundreds. If it is faulty, you've still only lost £20 and you'll probably make this up tenfold on your next purchase.

Following the viewing period is the registration period, in which you'll be required to provide details of your name and address, along with a refundable deposit of about £10 or £20. Registration is important as you'll be given your bidding card and number, which you'll need when bidding for anything. Registration is also a good time to make enquiries concerning VAT and any other additional charges.

The Bidding Procedure

By following these hints you'll avoid many of the pitfalls that can catch out newcomers.

1.   Observe at least two or three auctions before you become involved yourself.

2.   Spend a while examining the lots in the viewing time provided and make up your mind what you're after.

3.   Fix your budget. Decide how much you're prepared to bid and don't go beyond this limit. Exceeding your budget is the sign of an amateur. Don't feel pressured into paying over the odds for a lot, even if you feel it still represents a bargain.

4.   Don't accept the auctioneer's starting price. In most cases this will fall before the bidding properly begins.

5.   Be on your guard for people telling you the product you're bidding for is damaged or faulty. They may well be trying to put you off. Avoid being pressured out of a bidding war by ensuring you've thoroughly examined the lot beforehand. That way you can be sure of its quality.

6.   Be aware of "bidding off the wall". This is less common today and only occurs in less reputable houses. It involves the auctioneer raising the bid even though any competition has ceased. The newcomer is deceived into thinking they are still bidding against others and hence pays well over the odds.

7.   If you have your heart set on a lot, then wait until the bidding seems to be coming to an end. You can then interject your own bid and avoid a costly price war which could send the final amount spiralling upwards, way out of your reach.

        Whilst such devious tactics do occasionally occur, don't be put off. Most auctions follow correct procedures, making them bargain basements just waiting for you to snap up their incredible offers.

        As long as you have a decent knowledge of the bidding procedure and you've done your homework regarding the quality of the lot you're after, you will almost certainly come away with tremendous savings and a huge smile on your face.

Profit From Your Auction Bargains

You've returned from the auction and your lounge now resembles a Tandy's showroom. Don't worry. That hole in your wallet will soon be filled with cash, as you're about to make a huge profit on the bargains you've just purchased.

Classified Ads

The best way to unload the goods you now own is by advertising them in the classified section of your local paper. Because you paid so little for them in the first place, you can afford to sell them at discount prices and still make a fantastic profit. For example, a photocopier bought at auction for £250 might retail at £1,000 in a high street store. You can advertise it in the paper for between £600 and £750 and literally triple your investment.

Bicycles also offer a great investment opportunity. Hundreds of cycles are stolen daily, and even if the police recover them many people have already claimed on their insurance. You can find incredibly cheap racing and mountain bikes at auction which make great presents. By spending perhaps £60 on five or six cycles you could make hundreds by advertising them in the local paper before Christmas.

Other products commonly sold at auction which sell well through classifieds include computer equipment and games, antique furniture, TV, video, Hi-fi gear, fridges, washing machines, cookers and office or business equipment.

Trade Journals

If you've bought specialist goods (perhaps those photocopiers we mentioned earlier), try advertising them in trade magazines. Think how many small businesses are set up each day - they all need equipment but many won't be able to afford brand new goods. You will be providing massive discounts and still making large profits.

The same applies to vehicles purchased at auction. You really can find some terrific bargains, especially in the stolen and recovered lots. However, it is best to take a qualified mechanic with you to ensure the car is mechanically and structurally sound. By doing so, you can avoid lumbering yourself with a wreck that nobody wants. With expert advice you could pick up an ex-army Land Rover for between £200 to £300. You'll easily make nine or ten times that amount in a private sale.

By getting a feel for the right products to buy at auction and the prices to sell them on at, you can turn this buying and selling business into a real winner.

CHAPTER 15

STORE TO DOOR
A HOT NEW BUSINESS

Store to Door is a neat concept that is just waiting for someone in the UK to pick it up and run with it.

Much as we hate to admit it, those Yanks have great entrepreneurial flair. Here's a superb example of an ingenious idea being turned into a billion dollar business. A concept that entrepreneurs in Britain and elsewhere can copy!

The Store to Door Concept

This is how it works. Imagine Fred Smith wants to make his attic into a playroom for his grandchildren. The problem is, his attic is full of things like china, clothing, suitcases, fishing tackle, books and other assorted oddments.

Fred does not really use these possessions very often but he doesn't want to part with them. So instead he phones a specialist storage company, who arrange delivery of a container the size of a small garden shed to his home. Fred packs up the container himself. The firm returns and carries away the container to be stored in a warehouse until Fred wants his property back.

Fred pays a fee of about £40 a month for use of the storage container. If he ever wishes to check on his possessions, or wants to remove items from time to time, he pays a fee of say £10 per visit.

That's exactly how the concept works in the United States, where the self storage market is worth upwards of £9 billion dollars per annum. It shouldn't be difficult to tailor the idea to the UK market and achieve similar success.

Remember, this is a self storage business with a difference. What makes it unusual is that instead of the customer taking their items to the storage warehouse, the warehouse (or rather a container) comes to the customer. The container is dropped off at the client's address, filled by the client, and then picked up and deposited at the warehouse.

The convenience advantages are obvious.

Who Would Use The Service?

• The property market fluctuates dramatically. Many people have to sell their own home before they take possession of a new one. While relatives can often put them up, there is no room for the furniture.

• Students accumulate possessions they can't always take with them when they move or go away for the summer.

• We live on a crowded island. As a direct consequence of this houses are becoming smaller. There are few people who have the luxury of roomy attics or cellars. Given the option, many people would prefer to store their little used items rather than get rid of them.

• New firms move into premises that seem to be large enough at the time, but as the business expands, space becomes tight. It's cheaper to store unused items than it is to move into new premises.

• Any estate agent will tell you that a house which is free of clutter will sell more easily. It's not just that the house appears tidier, it also looks much larger. So anyone with a property to sell would be well advised to pack up any superfluous possessions until they move into their new home. Not only will their house sell more quickly, it will also make moving house less traumatic. Once the dust is settled, they can reclaim their possessions at their leisure.

Marketing The Enterprise

As mentioned earlier, the storage business in this country is largely untapped. What makes this one unique is that it gives clients the convenience of pick up and delivery. It doesn't matter how much convenience you can offer if no-one knows about you.

Here are a few promotional ideas.

• Get in touch with the Students Union and offer preferential rates to their members.

• Approach local estate agents. Explain to them how your business will increase their profits. You could draw up an agreement whereby an advertising leaflet is included with the valuation report which is forwarded to the vendor. Alternatively, post letters to anyone advertising their house in the property guides.

• Mailshot local businesses to let them know of your existence. Follow this up with a telephone call and arrange an appointment.

• Be alert to opportunities. Where does that cafe owner store his patio tables and chairs in the winter?

Though we've named just a few to get you started, the possibilities for promotion are endless.

To set this venture up from scratch would involve a hefty injection of capital and would carry a moderate risk I therefore would not recommend this business to anyone without experience of the transport or storage industry, unless they were to team up with someone with the necessary background.

That said, it is only a question of time before the idea of Store to Door storage takes off in this country in a big way. It is a genuine get rich opportunity, albeit not one for the dabbler. Marketed properly the business has the potential to take off in the UK as it has in the USA. I confidently predict that someone with a little vision will reap massive financial rewards.

In the UK, self-storage facilities such as Shurgard and Lock 'n' Store have been buying up and converting industrial units just as fast as they can - this is truly a massive growth area.

CHAPTER 16

MAKE MONEY AS A GREETINGS CARD DESIGNER

Discover how to set up your own profitable greetings card business from scratch. Cash in by making your own cards or by selling your designs to companies.

BE IT A BIRTHDAY or Christmas, Mother's Day or Father's Day, wedding or some other special event, you can be sure that someone is cashing in with a card to celebrate the moment.

In recent years the explosion in the numbers and styles of cards available has led to a boom in the card business, with many being produced and/or designed by home based enterprises.

Where a traditional card will contain a heart felt verse, modern greetings cards have rejected religious imagery and nature and replaced it with cynicism, dry humour and sex. The Purple Ronnie brand of cards, for instance, has had a profound impact on the market due to their light hearted perspective for any occasion.

Another successful area has been hand made cards. Their attractive design and 'one-off' nature makes them highly attractive. They are often made with recycled materials, giving them extra appeal with eco-friendly types, and they usually contain no message or wording, meaning they can be used for any occasion.

By developing an original idea for greetings cards you too could prosper from this continually growing market.

Contacting Card Companies

One option is to send your designs to major manufacturers, thus earning a regular commission for your work, or they may buy your ideas on a 'one off' basis. If suitably impressed, you may be offered freelance work or even a full time position. The Greeting Card Association (listed under Contacts) offers information regarding possible freelance work.

Though there are pitfalls, it's possible to earn a substantial amount by working for a greetings card manufacturer. Take the example of cartoonist Allan Plenderleith, whose break came when he submitted some comic strip ideas to Viz. While Viz didn't think his cartoons suited their particular brand of humour, they liked them enough to forward them to card publishers Emotional Rescue.

Allan struck lucky: the firm liked his designs and he walked away having sold 50 designs for £1,000. He was also awarded a regular contract. Allan is now writing an animation series based on his Odd Squad cartoons (a dysfunctional family featuring the characters Jeff, his 'big boned' girlfriend Maud, and parents Lily and Alf) which he plans to sell to Channel 4 or BBC2.

If you want to emulate Allan's success, contact card manufacturers with samples of your work. Cartoons featuring witty wordplay and strong characters are ideal. If your artistic skills aren't great, don't worry. A firm may simply purchase your 'concept' and hand it to a staff artist to produce the final design. Or you could get together with an artist and have them produce pictures to accompany your words.

Sadly, tales of card companies ripping off people's ideas are commonplace. The problem is that you can't copyright an idea - if you tell someone at the company about an idea for a range of cards you might have, and they then use the idea without paying you a penny for supplying it, you have no legal comeback.

Printed materials, on the other hand, can be copyrighted. The cheapest way to copyright your designs is to put them in an envelope, post them back to yourself by recorded delivery and store them unopened. That way you'll have sealed and dated copies of your work to prove the designs are yours. (Note that this still won't necessarily stop firms copying your designs - their financial muscle may be enough to deter small designers from challenging them in court.) when discussing your ideas with a company it's a good idea to have them sign a Confidentiality Agreement, meaning they agree not to pass on any of your ideas.

If you're considering working on a freelance basis then discuss ownership with the company in question. Generally you'd sign over the rights to an image, but you should establish exactly what your legal position will be.

Making Your Own Cards

Rather than signing away your designs and profits to a card company, a more practical route to success is to make and sell your own range of cards.

While it involves a little extra marketing effort, it's not difficult. You can copyright your own printed materials, meaning that card companies can't steal your designs. You can start small, working from home, and expand production as demand increases. Any profit, of course, goes straight into your pocket.

And there's always the chance that at a later date a big firm will spot your success and purchase your designs for a decent amount of money.

The materials you use and the equipment required depend on the kind of cards you're making. If you're making cards with a cartoon, caption, joke or message you can simply hand your original artwork to a printer, who will print up your designs in larger numbers. For an individual hand made card you can use any materials you like - beads, material, ribbons, glitter, pressed flowers or an original painting/drawing could be glued to coloured card to make an original design.

A good PC may be a worthwhile investment. With the right software it is possible to create, store and manipulate images/captions. A computer retailer will advise you on the best equipment to buy. You can even print cards direct from your hard disk using a top quality colour printer and printer compatible card, although if you are planning to produce your cards in bulk it is more economical to take them to a professional printer.

If you are making hand crafted cards you will also need to consider the costs of pens, pencils and artwork equipment as well as a guillotine. You may be able to purchase a guillotine second-hand for around £50.

Finally, don't forget the envelopes. These can be bought in bulk from wholesalers at a cost of around £30 for 1,000 envelopes.

Expect to spend at least £1,000 on your initial costs. This is necessary if you don't want your finished product to have the appearance of a market stall photocopy.

Getting Ideas

When searching for ideas it is a good idea to take a look at the racks in card shops to see what sells. Popular culture is a good source of inspiration. You will get some great ideas from adverts and magazine articles, but make sure you are not infringing any copyright laws by using other people's work.

The possibilities for style and content are limited only by your imagination. If you ensure your designs are original and eye catching you won't go far wrong. Risqué cards, featuring innuendo packed captions and suggestive images, tend to sell well, and computer art - fractals and eye catching abstract images - is popular too. If you are making individual cards by hand, ones containing an environmental or humanitarian message or image are always a big seller.

When it comes to pricing, take a look at what similar cards on the market sell for. Most retailers will expect to make a minimum of 50% profit, so aim to sell your designs for at least double the production costs. Mass produced cards generally retail for between £1 and £2. Individual, hand made cards are generally priced at between £1.50 and £5, reflecting the time and effort spent on creating a unique product.

Where to Sell Your Cards

Shops

Start by getting cards stacked in local shops and other outlets. Initially this may be on a sale or return basis, although if demand is sufficient, retailers may place a regular order. As sales increase you can progress to shops further away, promoting your wares to a wider audience and to larger retailers.

The kind of shops you approach will depend on the style of cards you produce. Usual outlets include card shops, newsagents, stationery shops, gift shops, art shops, book shops, department stores, market stalls and university shops.

For small, independent outlets you simply need to approach the shop manager. For large chain stores such as Woolworth and W H Smith you will need to seek out the person responsible for purchasing stock for the whole enterprise. Be tough and try to get as good a deal as possible. It might take just one major countrywide distribution deal to set you up for life.

Trade fairs and exhibitions

You can generate sales and interest for your cards by attending a trade fair/exhibition. They do not only cater for UK interest, but also attract the attention of overseas companies. The largest is an annual event known as The International Spring Fair, which attracts wholesalers and retailers from Europe and beyond. Unfortunately, due to the size of the event it is very difficult for a small scale, one man operation, to secure a stall. The places are limited and the costs are high. However, do not be disheartened - even if you cannot display your designs you can spend time talking to the major players and finding out useful contact addresses. Take a couple of examples of your work and hand out flyers. You may attract the attention of an interested party simply by being persistent.

Craft Fairs

Craft fairs up and down the country offer a great chance for newcomers to try out their designs on the general public. You will find event schedules in most craft shops, tourist information centres and local newspapers. Compile a portfolio of your designs to hand out to interested parties.

The Internet

By promoting your designs and taking credit card orders via the Internet you can take orders from around the world. One English store makes more money selling cards in Japan than it does from counter sales!

Magazine Features

You may be able to get a feature in a trade magazine. This will create great free publicity for your business and draw you to the attention of some important industry insiders. Contact trade and business related publications and ask if they would consider running a feature on you and your designs. They may wish to adopt a different angle than simply featuring a new designer. For example, you could propose a feature on the difficulties of getting your work recognised or the shifting trends in greeting card designs.

Expanding the Business

You may be happy working on your own, earning more than enough by supplying small, independent outlets locally. Do work hard on marketing and on obtaining a favourable deal with stockists, but equally, make sure you also allow enough time to work on your designs.

If any designs are not selling, try to discover why. It is a good idea to drop the less successful designs and concentrate your efforts on promoting the successful ones.

Ultimately though you may want to be in the position where you can supply cards in bulk to the whole country, or even internationally. Remember that W H Smith or whoever will need solid evidence that your cards are selling. You will also need to give serious consideration to your production methods - your kitchen table will no longer be suitable and you will have to consider taking on extra staff, moving to new premises and buying more equipment.

Alternatively, you may want to licence your designs to a major card manufacturer (basically meaning that they produce and market them, with profits being split). Although not necessarily as profitable as manufacturing them yourself, to a small card maker such as yourself it is a sign that you have made it, leaving you time to concentrate on new designs, take a holiday, perfect your golf swing

Remember, by designing witty, original pieces, it is possible to make a lot of money from greetings cards. Keep an eye on popular social trends and be able to manipulate these into marketable ideas for any occasion. You will also need to be tenacious and hard working. The current greeting card industry is dominated by large manufacturers like Fine Art and Carlton, making it difficult for small ventures to get their foot in the door.

However, if you can devise your own unique cards which will appeal to a broad cross section of the community, you may soon be receiving greeting cards from your new, millionaire friends.

Contacts

* *British Printing Industries Federation, 11 Bedford Row, London WC1R 4DX*
Tel: 020 7242 6904.
* *Greeting Card Association, 41 Links Drive, Elstree, London WD6 3P*
Tel: 020 8236 0024.
* *Greetings (Journal of the Greeting Card Association), Lema Publishing.*
Tel: 01923 250909.
* *London College of Printing and Distributive Trades, Elephant and Castle,*
London SE1 6SB.
Tel: 020 7514 6500.

CHAPTER 17

FOLDING SCOOTER TAXIS TAKE OFF!

DISCOVER HOW two entrepreneurs have made a success out of folding scooters

This is an exciting and innovative opportunity. Folding scooter taxis - an idea. Two young entrepreneurs are on the road to success, and their service has been acclaimed by the Design Council as one of the prestigious Millennium Products.

One For The Road was set up by 28 year old Alister Robinson and Jason James. They now employ 25 drivers at their two offices in Putney and Kennington, each of whom has a scooter that folds away into a bag which can be easily stored in a car boot.

This service is the answer for people who are worried about getting home after having a drink. Say someone has driven to a London show and decided to have a drink afterwards. They call up One For The Road, who send out a driver on his scooter. The driver reaches the customer on his scooter, then drives the customer home in the customer's own car, with the scooter stowed safely in the boot. When the customer's destination is reached the driver unpacks his scooter and heads off to the next person. Each driver, who must prove they are over 21 and have sufficient ability and street knowledge before they are taken on, is insured for up to £75,000 in case they damage a client's car.

The firm already has thousands of regular customers, who pay a set rate of £10 for up to three miles, plus a sliding charge for longer distances. While this is about 20% more than the cost of a one way cab fare, the customer is saved the hassle of collecting their car the next morning. They also escape the possibility of being clamped, or being fined and banned if they risk driving their vehicle home.

One problem James and Robinson had was obtaining suitable scooters, so they decided to design their own. Based on a Japanese monkey bike, their scooter has a four stroke engine and divides into two parts for easier stowing. The pair intend to import them and convert them in the UK. They have also done a deal with national Car Rentals to collect and deliver hire cars during the day - the perfect way to complement their evening activities and maximise profits.

CHAPTER 18

A CUT ABOVE THE REST
Starting a Press Cuttings Agency

Do you fancy earning money from sitting at home reading the paper? Well, that's how a press cuttings agent makes a living, cutting out articles from newspapers, filing them and sending them to their clients. Here's how to set up one of the simplest low cost, high profit businesses around.

Why is a Press Cuttings Agency Useful?

This is a business where you can turn old newspapers into cash. A simple newspaper or magazine article on the right subject is extremely useful to certain people, who pay press cuttings agents big money to send them on.

If you enjoy reading newspapers this will make a great second job, working part time in the evenings and weekends. Although if you market yourself in the right way and provide a good service, your press cuttings agency could grow into a profitable full time operation.

Where Do You Get Your Cuttings From?

Any printed matter is a potential source of clippings. Although which publications you read will depend on the subject and client, the main sources are as follows:-

National newspapers

Local newspapers (including freesheets)
Consumer publications
Trade, technical and professional journals
Company reports and magazines
Press releases

Current publications are listed, along with their addresses and phone numbers, in the Writers' and Artists' Yearbook, Benns, or Willing's Press Guide, available in libraries and book shops.

Potential Clients

There is a huge market for press clippings. The key to success is finding people who need them. The list includes the following.

PR Companies

Public relations companies need cuttings for two reasons. They need to know how (and how often) their clients are being portrayed in the media. They also need to prove to clients that their PR efforts are being picked up by the press. The more cuttings featuring their clients they can lay their hands on the better - they show them to clients as proof that their PR job is working.

Businesses

Many businesses handle their own publicity and will collect any published article that mentions themselves. Positive publicity might be mentioned in future advertising, whereas negative articles (for example, a report of record losses, a strike by workers, or a safety lapse) will be used as a record of details to overcome in future promotional campaigns. It is mainly larger businesses who use the services of cuttings agencies - others either don't bother monitoring their publicity or collect their own cuttings. Nevertheless it is a big market, and it is generally cheaper and less time consuming for firms to use a press cuttings agency rather than search for their own clippings. This is particularly the case with foreign companies who may find getting hold of UK publications too difficult or expensive. Press reports and ads relating to other companies are useful market intelligence as they may provide possible sales leads, marketing examples, and competitor information.

Other Organisations

All manner of organisations require press clippings, for similar reasons to the above. You might, for instance, be asked by a theatre company to collect reviews of a touring play, or by a charity to collect cuttings featuring fund raising exploits.

Other press clipping agencies

You may be able to subcontract work from other press clipping agencies. You could take on work when they are busy, for example. Or, they may ask you to cover specific subject areas or publications for them.

These are your main potential clients. However, there are other ways of making money from the snippets you collect.

Getting Started

Now you have an idea of the size and profitability of the market for press clippings, it is time to learn how to run the business. I have already listed the main potential sources of press cuttings.

Ideally you want to find a client, find the right publications, and then start collecting clippings. In reality things won't be that simple. You'll probably need to establish yourself as a quality cuttings agent in order to convince anyone to use your service, so a more proactive approach to finding clients will be needed.

In other words, you will need to start collecting cuttings before you have found any clients. These can then be passed on to potential customers as proof of how good your service is, which may convince them to hire you. Other articles can be filed away until required in the future, either by a client, or by yourself as source materials for a book or article. A glance at the racks of any newsagent will indicate the massive range of possible sources for cuttings. Simply buying up the necessary publications will be far too expensive, and there are any number of possible subjects you might want to cover. So where do you begin?

Collecting Source Materials

Rather than buying up as many publications as you can afford, start by collecting recently discarded newspapers. Approach friends, neighbours and workplaces and ask if you can collect their old newspapers on a regular basis. Hotels and cafes often buy in a selection of papers for their customers, so it is well worth trying these places.

Another source of articles is your local library, which will keep all the main newspapers, periodicals and magazines. There's nothing to stop you photocopying anything you are interested in. Again, this may save you the expense of buying new publications.

As well as having somewhere to store the newspapers and articles, you need to consider what subjects you are going to concentrate on, since you can't cover everything. Stick to:-

1.   Things which might have saleable value (see *Potential Clients*), and
2.   Things you are interested in.

Obviously, any client or potential market will determine the subjects you choose to cut out.

Cutting and Filing Articles

Once you've decided what subjects to cover, obtain some A4 envelopes and write your subject headings on them. Example headings might be the Royal Family, Cliff Richard, or the Vauxhall Motor Company. Next, scan each publication systematically, cut out any article mentioning your subject, and place it in the relevant envelope. These envelopes are then filed in alphabetical order until needed.

Each cutting must be labelled - either write the publication name and date on the back of the article, or glue the cutting to some plain A4 paper and type on the publication and date. The better presented your cuttings are, the more professional the image you will give customers.

Marketing and Promotion

When your envelopes are nice and full, start sending example cuttings to potential clients. Your sales approach should stress that your service is professional and inexpensive, and that you have plenty more cuttings available. Be persistent - with a bit of luck they will decide to use your services. They may pay you for a one off selection of articles or hire you on an ongoing basis. If they don't bite, either continue cutting and filing articles or amend your subject headings, depending on whether you feel the cuttings are saleable.

At this stage it is well worth taking out advertising. Because most cutting agencies are based in London you could find it advantageous to concentrate on advertising and getting clients in your local area, as there may be less competition. Start by sending out sales letters to PR agencies. Also, put a small, cheap, classified ad in local papers on a regular basis - something like: "Press cuttings service available covering all subjects", plus your name and address. There are many publications offering low cost or free ads, such as the Writers and Artists Yearbook, so get ads in as many of these as possible. When you have more cash behind you obtain listings in the Yellow Pages and Thomson Local.

Although things might be slow at first, which is why we have explained the cheapest method of getting started, in time you should build up some profitable regular clients. At this stage your job will become easier. You will know exactly what subjects to look for and which publications to find them in, so it will simply be a case of cutting and sending off articles as required. With a bit of luck your income will be enough to buy new papers and magazines rather than collecting them off your mates and hanging around the public library.

Set your fees competitively to cover stationery costs and other expenses and provide a reasonable profit. To get an idea of what to charge, contact other cutting agencies (under your own name, not your business name) and ask for a rate card.

Conclusion

Although this isn't the most exciting business in the world, anyone who reads a lot will enjoy it, and the market for press cuttings is bigger than you probably first thought. There are plenty of income possibilities from working for clients to sending off snippets and publishing your own articles and books. This is why established self employed agents can earn over £20,000 a year.

Best of all it is a low risk service that you can start from your own armchair, working evenings and weekends, with the potential to become your main source of income. So what are you waiting for - get cutting!

More Money Making Uses For press Clippings

Sending snippets
British publications are interested in news stories from the rest of the world, especially celebrity gossip, funny or bizarre stories, or scandals. There is a lucrative market in passing on these snippets. Tabloid style publications such as the national Enquirer in the US are ideal for such stories. Fan clubs, collectors and hobbyists may pay for snippets relating to certain people.

Publish your own books and articles

There's nothing to stop you using the information collected in your files as the basis of a book or article along the lines of '25 things you didn't know about ...', or '50 royal scandals'. You could sell articles to magazines or publish a book yourself. Celebrities, pop stars and the royal family offer the best scope for such articles, although there are all kinds of possible themes.

CHAPTER 19

FOOD FOR THOUGHT

CATERING AND COOKING OPPORTUNITIES

EVERYONE HAS TO EAT, so there's always a gap in the market for a new catering business or food product. Look at the number of catering businesses in your area, and at the number of new food products on the supermarket shelves: proof that someone is making big money.

Catering and cooking aren't areas that necessarily require great skills. Anyone who can make a sandwich or a cup of tea could earn money simply by being in the right place at the right time.

Nor do you need to invest in expensive cooking apparatus. There are plenty of catering businesses that people run successfully from the comfort of their homes, using basic kitchen utensils. When equipment is required there are ways to minimise the cost, such as buying second-hand or reconditioned goods.

Here are our top 20 catering and cooking opportunities, guaranteed to whet the appetite of any aspiring entrepreneur.

Sandwich Making

One of the simplest and most lucrative catering opportunities is sandwich making. Setting up a stall or shop near local businesses will guarantee substantial passing lunchtime trade. Workers snatching a bite to eat during their lunch break represent a virtually captive market, so the closer your premises to large firms and the less competition there is nearby, the higher the prices you can charge.

Offer a basic range of items initially, preparing the fillings and buttering the rolls in readiness for the lunchtime rush. You can offer drinks and other snacks too, such as crisps and fruit, or even hot pies and pasties if you have a microwave oven handy. Try to gauge the tastes of your customers - you may want to provide more exotic and/or health oriented sandwiches if your customers are affluent office workers.

Since the main bulk of your trade is around lunchtime you need only open for a few hours a day, so this is an ideal part time operation. The great thing about sandwich making is that you don't need much in the way of catering equipment and the basic ingredients are easy and inexpensive to buy in bulk. Don't forget that - as with any other catering business - you must keep your kitchen, your clothes and yourself spotlessly clean.

Mobile Catering

Instead of preparing food in your kitchen, why not take the kitchen with you? Things like fish and chip vans, hot dog and kebab stalls, and coffee and tea stands all make money because they are able to set up close to their customers. Outside shopping centres and markets, close to crowds at sports events and concerts, next to pubs and clubs at closing time, at the beach or park, at a car boot sale .... you can set up anywhere with a good flow of people.

You'll need some form of mobile stall or van, kitted out with the necessary food preparation equipment. This might include an oven, griddle or deep fat fryer, or simply a sink and kettle. Vehicles are often advertised in publications such as Exchange and Mart, the Trader, and Market Trader, or you could buy a franchise.

Alternatively, you could purchase an old van, caravan or small bus and convert it into a mobile kitchen yourself. Once armed with a vehicle, plus the necessary licences, you can seek out your customers. Where you go is up to you, but if you're there on the same days and times you'll build up regular custom.

CATERING : LEGAL REQUIREMENTS

THERE ARE VARIOUS LEGAL REQUIREMENTS for anyone operating a catering related business:

* You must register all food premises with your local council Environmental Health department at least 28 days before you start trading, according to the 1991 Food Premises Regulations. These details are held for public inspection by your local authority.

* You may need a catering licence - the requirements vary from place to place, but your council Environmental Health, Commercial Services and/or Trading Standards department will inform you of the local regulations.

If you intend to employ anyone else in your business there are further considerations:

* Anyone who handles food must receive appropriate training, according to the 1995 Food Safety Regulations.

* You will also need Employer's Liability Insurance - you must display the certificate on your premises at all times.

Food on Foot

Another option is to do without a vehicle and carry your food or drinks on foot. If you seek out crowds - people waiting in queues, or spectators at a concert or football match for example - you have a captive market to sell to. If it's the middle of summer you can sell cold drinks, and if it's winter you can sell warm pies and pasties. Snacks, sweets and sandwiches will sell well anytime.

The advantage of being on foot is that you can move around the crowds easily, to places a van couldn't get to, selling to customers who may be hungry or thirsty but can't make it to a shop. You can charge high prices for this reason. To hold your goods you'll need some form of insulated bag that you can carry on your back comfortably for long periods. A bike may be useful for getting from place to place, or to fetch more stock.

Pub Cooking

Pubs are getting increasingly involved in selling food, as it helps to attract punters and is highly profitable. Not all landlords have the time, experience, inclination or staff to be able to offer an enticing range of meals and bar snacks. So there are opportunities for enterprising caterers to take on the catering on behalf of local pubs.

Whether you are paid by the brewery or run it as your own separate business (with you taking the profits and paying the pub a commission) is up to you, but the pub will benefit from being able to offer food, and so will you.

Vegetarian Catering

Vegetarianism is becoming increasingly popular in the UK. Although most restaurants realise this and provide non meat options, there are still gaps in the market for vegetarian and vegan food. Setting up a vegetarian cafe or restaurant could be hugely popular in the right area, attracting meat eaters who want to sample something different as well as vegetarians who aren't catered for locally.

To increase profitability it is worth providing a delivery service, or perhaps selling pre-cooked packaged meals via other outlets. Other than word of mouth, useful promotional methods involve advertising in health food shops, putting up small ads or posters in shop windows and on notice boards, and even direct mailing. Since more people now realise that vegetarian food can be imaginative and exciting as well as healthy and nutritious, this is a growing market.

Tasty Takeaways

A portion of chips, a pizza, a kebab ...... chances are you'll have eaten at least one of these in the last week. This kind of takeaway food is big business, which is exactly why you see so many chippies, pizza parlours and kebab houses along the high street. There is always room for more! By purchasing second-hand equipment - or even a franchise - and finding a good site, you can soon set up a top takeaway that does a roaring trade with lunchtime business people and passing pub customers.

Party Catering

People love to put on lavish parties to entertain and impress friends and family, which means they will spare no expense in providing their guests with top quality cuisine. There are opportunities for outgoing entrepreneurs to take on the catering for these events. First you'll need to liaise with clients to discuss their requirements: the number of guests; possible menu; drinks; seating, tables, cutlery, glasses, plates and so on; and the client's budget.

You may need to hire equipment and staff, and book entertainment. On the day you must prepare and serve the food - you might require assistance with cooking, waiting on tables and washing up - clear up afterwards, and ensure all goes to plan. This requires co-ordination as well as cooking skills, but you can charge premium prices for this all inclusive service (of course, the client may just want you to supply and deliver the food ready cooked). Word of mouth recommendations are the best way to get clients, but it is worth advertising in shop windows and local papers initially.

Themed Banquets

Putting on parties with a special theme - a medieval banquet, a Roman orgy or a Wild West night - is a fun alternative to the usual party catering. You'll need to produce an appropriate menu, and hire and organise the venue, entertainment, costumes, waiting staff, cutlery, and so on.

It's a good idea to market this service to businesses, since they often have social events to entertain clients and customers, motivate the sales team, or reward loyal staff, and will pay highly to have a themed event organised for them.

Confectionery Making

Sweets will always sell, especially if they are home made. If you have the know-how, making confectionery - chocolates, toffee, fudge, mints and boiled sweets - is something you can do in your own kitchen. It's a good idea to personalise the sweets in some way. By using special packaging, using lettering made from fondant icing, or even shaping them in a particular way, you can link them to the village, town or city, or a local attraction or beauty spot. The home made and the personalised elements will combine to make your products perfect for local gift shops and the like, selling at premium prices.

Although the market will primarily be local retailers, if your sweets fill a certain niche you may be able to sell them nationally or even internationally, either through chain stores or by mail order. The alternative is to sell your wares yourself at markets, craft fairs, fetes, exhibitions, boot sales, and so on.

Baking Cakes

Making cakes is the quintessential kitchen table business. There is a ready market for celebration cakes, for birthdays, christenings, anniversaries and - most profitably - weddings. Make (or buy) either sponge or fruit bases, then use fondant icing to produce innovative designs that relate to your client's interests - a car shaped one for an auto enthusiast, or a football shaped one for a football fan, for example.

There are plenty of books available that will teach you the art of cake making and decorating, and will feature designs you can copy. You can sell a typical sponge birthday cake for about £10, a fruit anniversary cake for £15, and a three tier wedding cake for up to £50. Advertise in local shop windows and persuade local bakers and grocers to act as your agent - create a brochure from photos of previous creations and have it placed on their counters.

Cooking for Kids and Babies

Teatime can be traumatic for many parents when their offspring won't eat what they have been given. Kids' tastes are extremely fickle, but they tend to prefer sweet and unhealthy foods rather than vegetables or fruit. Any product that becomes popular among children is likely to be extremely lucrative.

The way to become a hit with tender taste buds is to create sweet and/or strong tasting items with a fun element, using brightly coloured packaging, perhaps with drawings and cartoons. If you can make the products healthy as well as fun, they will be a hit with mums and dads too. If you have got a food processor you could create a range of baby food - the healthy home-made image will make it a hit with concerned parents.

Creating Speciality Sauces

Speciality cooking sauces have all the hallmarks of the ideal product: cheap to make, and selling for a high profit mark up. All sorts of varieties could be made using either home grown or locally bought produce (even if this means your local wholesaler) - salad dressings, spicy ethnic sauces, tomato and basil based pasta sauces, wild herb based sauces for meat, fish and salads, for example.

Great recipes turn up all over the place, although if you have your own special one, so much the better. Get your sauces stocked in delicatessens and supermarkets, or sell by mail order to boost profits.

Speciality Snacks

Another thriving sector is speciality snacks. The advent of kettle chips and gourmet crisps has breathed life into the snack sector, and shows how adding an innovative slant to an already established item can create a massively successful product.

Start small if you wish, perhaps producing potato, corn, nut, dried fruit or muesli based snacks in your kitchen and selling them through local retailers or by yourself on a market stall. If you can personalise them in some way, or find a particular demand niche, you will do well. Low fat and healthy items are becoming very popular.

Organic Foods

The increase in healthy eating, coupled with the environmental damage caused by man made fertilisers and insecticides, has led to a growth in demand for organic produce. A range of foods, drinks or cooking ingredients made from organically grown produce is likely to be a high earner. Health food shops are an obvious market, although if you are more ambitious you could get your products stocked in supermarket chains, or sell them by mail order.

Cheese

Traditionally made cheese is the kind of product that goes down a storm with food lovers, who will pay highly for it in delicatessens, cheese shops and the more upmarket supermarket counters. Cheese made locally in small amounts has far more character than the mass produced factory made brands, and hence sells at higher prices.

You might want to buy or make wooden churns and use old fashioned techniques to make your products. This is a rewarding part time operation that has the potential to become your main income earner.

Sausages

Sausages are another popular food you can make yourself at home. The average customer would rather eat a tasty sausage made from local products using traditional methods than a bland mass produced variety. Of course, you can sell your product at a higher price, giving you a healthy profit margin, and still give your customers value for money. As well as getting them stocked in butchers shops and delis, try getting local restaurants to put them on their menu - it will be good publicity.

Pickled Foods

Top quality gourmet pickles hand made from the finest ingredients - chillies, oranges, ginger, figs and beer - are likely to be a big hit with discerning customers. Pickling foods, putting them in jars and adding your own brand sticker is something you could easily do from home. Obtain a book or two on the subject from your library and start practising. Practically anything can be pickled, so if you pick the right product and the right recipe this could prove profitable!

Pet Foodstuffs

If your culinary efforts prove unfit for human consumption, why not sell it as pet food? Seriously, there are possibilities for using cheaply made/purchased ingredients and repackaging it for pets. Nuts can be placed in net bags and sold as bird feeders, or you could bake cakes made from bird seed. Meat offcuts could be recycled as quality dog and cat food, and bones, ears and tails used as dog chews. Pet shops and hardware stores are the obvious sales options.

Devising Recipes and Cookery Books

Like most things, if you are particularly good at something you can make money from teaching others how to do it. Cookery books are no exception. Why not gather together some recipes you have devised yourself and publish them as a book? A simple 20 page photocopied booklet sold for a few pounds will suffice, although if you use photographs and get the book professionally printed you can charge more and earn more money on each book.

If you're a real culinary expert, you could film an instruction video. Your books/videos could be sold on a mail order basis and/or sold in book shops, food stores and gift shops.

Further Information

- *Mobile and Outside Caterers Association - Tel: 0121 693 7000*
- *Ministry of Agriculture, Fisheries and Food - Tel: 020 7270 8080*
- *Department of Agriculture (Northern Ireland) - Tel: 01232 524392*
- *HMSO (have a range of booklets covering food laws) - Tel: 020 7233 0011*

- *Food From Britain (deals with food exports and the development of speciality food and drink businesses in the UK) - Tel: 020 7233 5111*
- *Welsh Food Promotion - Tel: 01222 640456*
- *Scottish Enterprise - Tel: 0141 248 2700*

CHAPTER 20

QUICK START SECURITY BUSINESSES

With more than one house broken into every minute, burglary now accounts for over one in five recorded crimes. Here are 20 low cost, high profit, opportunities to earn money by making people feel more safe, happy and secure.

SAFETY AND SECURITY IS MORE OF A PRIORITY THAN EVER. Last year there were over 600,000 reported burglaries in England and Wales alone. Unfortunately, the police clear up rate is less than one case in four, so the need for people to consider preventative measures is paramount.

Happily, there are many low cost businesses you could start in order to capitalise on the demand for security related products and services. Here are 20 ideas, from modest part time earners to full time independent enterprises, from which you can secure your own financial future.

1.   Private Protection Patrol

Burglary and violence are a threat in practically every neighbourhood, but the police just don't have the resources to keep a constant eye on everybody's property, or even every street. One way to offer a little extra peace of mind to locals is to set up a private patrol service.

A fit and vigilant retiree with their own vehicle would be perfect for this. It involves driving slowly past the houses enrolled on the scheme at least once every two hours to check for intruders, while at the same time acting as a deterrent to crime. You'll need a CB radio link with someone else who can telephone the police for assistance when you spot anything suspicious.

This service will be particularly lucrative in areas inhabited by working couples whose homes will be vacant during the day, presenting an easy target for thieves. You could provide an additional service for people away on holiday - homeowners could leave their keys for you to check the inside of their houses, tidy up the post and even feed the pets. Sign 50 people to your scheme, charge them £15 a month each for the basic service, and you'll generate a monthly income of £750.

Note that you have no powers of arrest and you are not in any way replacing the police. However, you will be providing much needed extra security in the neighbourhood.

2.   Fitting Window Locks and Bars

It's all too easy for a determined burglar to gain entrance to a property by smashing a window or jemmying it open. For households the best solution is to fit window locks, while window bars may be more suitable for business properties.

You could cash in from fitting these items. As well as the products themselves, which you can buy from a wholesaler or directly from the manufacturer, you will need a ladder, electric drill with regular and masonry bits, masonry anchors, one-way screws and assorted tools.

Target customers by distributing attractive leaflets informing them of the need for your service. Aim to speak personally with the householder/manager to get a firm commission.

3.   Nanny Surveillance

Despite being found not guilty, the Louise Woodward case has made parents more wary of employing a child minder. However, there is often no alternative should they wish to pursue a career.

There is a service already establishing itself in the US, which can allay parents' fears. With the use of a small video camera and a remote video recorder it is possible to monitor a nanny while they are at work. In America people are buying this equipment and making money from setting it up in parents' homes, while keeping an eye on the nanny to ensure they can be trusted. The concept will be in demand here too.

Suppliers of surveillance/CCTV systems include:-
*   Digital Systems UK, London (Tel: 020 8668 0101)
*   JJN Electronics, London (Tel: 020 8508 9701)
*   Merlin Surveillance, Middlesex (Tel: 020 8362 1111)
*   Qtek Products, Middlesex (Tel: 01474 355050)
*   21st Century CPS, Blackburn (Tel: 01254 697989)
*   Leeds Spy Centre (Tel: 0113 230 2000)
*   Manchester Spy Centre (Tel: 0161 766 1244)
*   Manchester Surveillance Company (Tel: 0161 205 9636).

4.   Insurance Videotaping

Items particularly at risk in household robberies include jewellery, TVs, VCRs, Hi-Fis and computers. When they are stolen, people sometimes have a hard time obtaining the insurance money because they find it difficult to prove they actually owned the items claimed for. The insurance video service is another one popular in the US with potential in the UK. Camcorder owners will film clients' possessions in their homes. The client keeps one copy of the video and the original is handed to the insurance company as a record. If you own a camcorder this could be for you - approach insurance companies directly and/or advertise in local newspapers to get work.

5. Be A Locksmith

Since the persistent thief's aptitude for cracking locks improves with each passing year there is a need for increasingly sophisticated locks to keep them out. By doing a little training as a locksmith you'll have a useful extra string to your bow and will be able to make money anywhere. Try your careers library or ask at specialist lock shops about courses.

You can advise people on the correct locks to install, and then fit them. This niche service commands fees of over £50 an hour, plus expenses.

6. Outdoor Light Installation

Those shady nooks and crannies outside your house provide perfect cover for crooks and other assorted ne'er-do-wells. You can now obtain bright yet economical lighting systems (including timer controlled devices and infra red laser operated lights which respond to an intruder's movement to illuminate those outdoor passages, back yards, gardens and garages.

Electrically minded types could tap into the demand for fitting these products in homes and businesses via a campaign of door to door handouts, ads in the local paper or Yellow Pages, and postcards in shop windows.

7. Fitting Burglar Alarms

The rising crime rate has led to a boom in the burglar alarm market. Few firms would be without one, and the majority of private homes either already have one or are considering getting one fitted.

A security alarm business has potential anywhere. If you wanted you could run this as a part time venture, fitting alarms on evenings and weekends.

Suppliers of alarms can be tracked down through business directories and mail order magazines. While you'll need to familiarise yourself with how the systems work, this shouldn't take long. Household alarms are simpler than commercial alarms and fitting them is something the average handyman can do, with a little thought and skill.

Nobody will buy a burglar alarm from a cowboy type operation, so the number one rule is to maintain a professional, upstanding image at all times. Use good quality letterheads and promotional materials, pay attention to the appearance of your office and personal attire, and be on hand to offer in depth advice and assistance on all of your products.

Press advertising and leaflets are the obvious means of promotion - get an extra edge by offering free surveys and quotes.

Household burglar alarms usually cost £200 to £1,000 to supply and fit. This can be anywhere from three and ten times the cost of the parts, so you can imagine how profitable this is.

8.   Selling Security Devices

If you're no good with your hands you could sell security products, rather than install them. That includes anything with security or safety potential, door viewers, safes, personal anti attack alarms, fire and smoke alarms, fire extinguishers, padlocks, door chains, car alarms, and all the other products mentioned in this article.

Companies are a valuable market. You could also get trade from homeowners by targeting Neighbourhood Watch groups and holding free seminars on home security. Combine this with newspaper and Yellow Pages ads and/or personalised mailshots.

9. Home Security Service

Readers who consider themselves experts on security could make money as a consultant, visiting homeowners and advising them on ways to make their properties more safe and secure. The going rate will be at least £20 per visit.

Make sure you're in a position to supply and fit the equipment necessary to bring their premises up to scratch. Offer to refund the cost of the consultation if they order directly from you.

10. PC Security

To a firm, having its PCs stolen would be costly and a major inconvenience. What if it lost its customer database or had secret product information stolen by a competitor? The potential loss would be immeasurable, which is why companies need to wise up to the benefits of PC security.

Selling and installing PC security systems is something anyone with a basic knowledge of computers could get into. Simply target small to medium sized firms and convince them of the benefits.

Savtec (Tel: 01420 541370) stocks a range of PC security kits designed to lock computer hardware to a fixed surface, thus preventing theft and unauthorised use. Portable disk drives and CD writers are another essential security option. They allow the user to keep a back up of their computer files in case they are stolen or the office burns down.

11.   Commercial Surveillance

Surveillance is an important area of security, with business surveillance being especially lucrative. Industry is awash with tales of staff stealing cash, pilfering stock, and/or forging invoices over a long period.

Industrial espionage is a big problem too. Businesses have been bankrupted when a departing employee has leaked their client list or top secret product information to a competitor, or has used it to set up their own enterprise.

When this happens, firms will call upon a private detective experienced in surveillance techniques to seek out the culprits. This might be done using a combination of undercover work (perhaps the PI and their associates will disguise themselves as fellow employees) and the use of sophisticated monitoring hardware (things like phone taps, transmitters and covert recording devices).

It's a fascinating area. Opportunities are expanding as firms realise that paying a private detective £500 a day is small beer when compared with how much they can save.

To get involved in this your best option is to take a specialised course in private investigation - commercial surveillance and private investigation. By the time you complete the course you will have sufficient information to trade as a private investigator.

12.   Business Security Service

Prevention is better than cure when it comes to commercial security, especially when you consider that stock, cash and information losses can cost a firm millions of pounds. This advisory service is a spin-off from the previous opportunity.

Start by conducting a study of the firm, its premises, processes, assets and staff, and advise on areas where internal security may be improved. After that your task will be to visit once a month to check up on security procedures. Although useful in itself, your presence will also be an excellent deterrent to petty crime.

Charge a few hundred pounds for the initial analysis, plus another few hundred (renegotiated on an annual basis) for the monthly visits.

13. Become A Store Detective

Store detection is another specialised area of commercial surveillance. While larger stores tend to employ full time store detectives, private detectives are increasingly hired on a temporary, freelance basis for this kind of work.

Again, the way to make money as a freelance store detective is to take a course in private investigation.

14. Nightwatchman or Security Guard

Anyone trained as a Private Investigator will be well placed to earn good money as a freelance security guard. The basic nightwatchman's job requires no qualifications at all, but involves working unsociable hours, can be boring and lonely, and generally is not well paid. So why not set up an agency supplying nightwatchmen to factories, offices and the like?

By recruiting trustworthy people and convincing companies to use your service you can pay your staff a reasonable wage and still make a hefty profit, without doing the actual work yourself.

15. Be A Bodyguard

You can earn up to £200 a day as a bodyguard. As well as protecting celebrities, bodyguards are commonly hired to accompany wage collections, protect cash and valuables, and escort businessmen on trade missions. It is best to be prepared for just about anything.

Beyond giving out business cards and getting a Yellow Pages or Thomson Local Directory listing, bodyguards and their agents do not really advertise. Instead they get work through recommendations from satisfied clients. Some are awarded permanent contracts, or set up their own agencies.

Finding initial clients takes persistence, but business usually builds from there.

16.   Lost Key Service

Losing a key is a troublesome prospect for most people. As well as the inconvenience there is the worry of it ending up in the hands of someone with less than honest intentions.

It is obviously not a good idea for anyone to leave their address on their keys. The solution? A lost key service. Each client is issued with a key fob which says something like, "If found, please return to Anytown Lost Key Service, PO Box XXX £10 reward for return". So the finder has an incentive to return the keys and the owner knows they are not going to get burgled.

Charge clients £25 a year (with a surcharge if they lose their keys more than once). Get 200 clients and you will earn £5,000 a year, which will be barely dented by paying out for marketing expenses, key fobs and the occasional reward.

17.   Keyholding Service

If you are reliable and can cope with being called out in the middle of the night, you can make money as a keyholder for local businesses. If the alarm goes off during the night for any reason it is you who the alarm company telephones. You must go out, check the property over and ensure the premises are fully secure before you leave.

It makes sense for firms to employ a keyholder for two reasons. Firstly, alarm companies often have trouble locating the firm's keyholder. Records may not have been updated, or the person responsible may have gone on holiday.

Secondly, 90% of callouts are false alarms, triggered by wind, rain, thunder or traffic. No working person wants their night's sleep ruined, so firms will be prepared to pay someone else to check the premises. Charge an annual on call fee of at least £100 per firm.

18.   House Sitting

The best way to protect property and possessions when away on holiday is to have someone else living there, which is why house sitting has become so popular. Through an agency, clients will book someone to look after the house, air the rooms, water the plants, feed the pets and even take the dog for a walk. Though there is no reason why you can't set up an independent service, the best way to get work as a house sitter is to contact an agency such as Homesitters (Tel: 01296 630730) or Housewatch (Tel: 01279 777412). While average earnings are a modest £40 a week, it is easy work. Recently retired couples are particularly well suited.

19.   Goosy Guardians

This might seem an odd idea, but if you have ever heard a goose screech you will understand how good a security device they can be. Geese are so effective at sounding the alarm when encountering intruders that one world famous whisky producer has pressed them into service as guards.

This ancient idea is rapidly regaining popularity. A goose is much cheaper than an electric alarm and has the fringe benefit of being able to supply eggs for breakfast. Anyone who can breed and/or supply geese can expect up to £50 a bird.

20.   Renting Lock-Up Space

If you have a garage or unused shop or warehouse space you don't use, you could make money by turning it into a secure lock-up area. Firms, individuals, and even the local council will be interested.

Complete security is one selling point. Only the client holds a key, so their privacy is assured. Convenience is the other major attraction. Imagine that Firm X has one main storage area on the south side of town where workers (cleaners, for example) have to visit to collect their equipment before they do the job, and drop it off again when they finish. It would make sense for Firm X to lease a second small storage area in the north of town to make things easier for staff who live and work in that area, saving them a journey across town.

You could charge £100 a month per ten cubic feet of space. By dividing, say, a garage into three separate lock-ups, you could earn £300 a month for no effort at all.

CHAPTER 21

MAKE A FORTUNE FROM YOUR OWN INVENTION

Following in the footsteps of the famous inventors who have made millions from their products is something we all dream about. It may take time, money and persistence to turn an idea into reality, but anyone can do it. Here's how.

"I will invent something........ then I'll become a millionaire!" This is something we've probably all thought about at some point.

All you have to do is come up with an ingenious idea for a new product, patent it, license it to a manufacturer and watch the millions roll in when your invention turns out to be a big seller in the shops. Simple!

In fact, making money from your own invention can be a difficult and drawn out process. Individuals take out some 4,000 patents a year, yet only 2% of these products ever reach the shops. There are plenty of pitfalls for aspiring inventors to watch out for, including the expense of development costs and the arduous process of applying for a patent.

Things may be getting easier - last October the Patent Office scrapped the £25 initial patent filing fee. You can take heart from the success stories.

Famous Stories of Success

Take Ron Hickman, inventor of the famous Workmate Home DIY Workbench. Sales of his product have run into millions world-wide since Black and Decker picked up on his idea, and he became a multimillionaire years ago thanks to the royalties he receives on each sale.

Then there's James Dyson's legendary bagless vacuum cleaner. Unlike other vacuum cleaners, his does not use waste bags, which are costly and fiddly to replace. While it took years and no little expense to develop the product, Dyson is now able to bask in the fame and fortune his brainwave has brought him.

Inventor's Step-by-Step Guide

If you've got some bright ideas and want to make millions from your own invention, here's what to do.

1.   Document Your Idea

Once inspiration has struck, make drawings that show what your invention is, how it works, the design, what materials might be used, and its advantages.

Keep the idea secret until you've filed the patent application. If your idea has already been made public the patent may not be granted.

2.   Apply For A Patent

A patent gives you ownership of your invention for up to 20 years, and means that no-one can make, sell or import your invention or make money from it without your permission. You can grant the right to someone else to make, sell or import it. Most inventors make money by licensing their inventions to another company, rather than manufacturing the product themselves.

The Patent Office will provide the application forms and offer guidance on the patent application procedure. Basic Patent Office fees are £200. The whole process, from the patent being filed to being granted, takes over two and a half years, but there is now a fast track system available that takes under a year.

You can save money by filing the patent yourself, but this can be tricky and time consuming. Your right to make money from the patent may be jeopardised if it hasn't been properly written up. The alternative is to use a chartered patent agent, who will file a professionally written patent for around £600 to £1,000.

The Chartered Institute of Patent Agents will put you in touch with a reputable agent. Bear in mind that international patents will be required if you intend to sell your invention abroad.

3.   Ensure The Invention Is Original

For the patent to be accepted you must prove that your idea is genuinely original and not based upon an existing product. It is possible to check in advance of filing by using a patent agent or search bureau, which will cost around £650 - £700.

4.   Find A Manufacturer

Once patented, it is time to look for a firm who can sell or license your invention (unless you are in a position to make and sell it yourself).

Seek out manufacturers who make similar products to yours. Approach the largest firms first - they are constantly on the lookout for new patents to buy and may reward you with a hefty cheque.

To keep costs down, try to find a buyer or licensee within the first year. If you can't find a UK manufacturer try extending your search to include overseas firms.

5.   Try Using A Technology Broker

A technology broker can be useful in your search for a manufacturer.

For an upfront fee (typically £2,000 - £4,000) they will assist in marketing your invention, which commonly involves printing promotional materials and approaching firms on your behalf.

You should beware though - many technology brokers offer a poor return on your investment and produce promotional materials that are low quality and/or contain only generalised information. Don't use any broker who cannot supply a reference. The more dubious take out adverts in the press with such headlines as 'Inventions Wanted.' Avoid. The Patent Office offers advice on finding a reputable broker.

Inventions fairs are a practical - and less expensive - method of meeting interested manufacturers. You can swap tips with fellow inventors too. About £400 is the going rate for your own stand.

6.   Get A Confidentiality Agreement Signed

Don't talk to any manufacturer until they have signed a confidentiality agreement. This ensures they won't steal or reveal your idea.

While people commonly pay a solicitor to draw one up, you can do it yourself. Your local business library will have details of model contracts you can use for this purpose.

7.   Get The Best Deal Possible

You usually have two options for selling and licensing your invention. You could negotiate a one off fee with the highest bidder. Or more likely, you will be offered a royalty deal combining a small up front payment (usually between £500 and £5,000) with a sales royalty worth around 2% to 7% of either the retail price or the manufacturing cost.

Don't simply accept the first offer that comes along though - shop around for the best deal and check the small print on every contract you sign. A patent agent will advise whether or not a particular deal is fair.

Make Money From Your Brainchild

Remember, having the idea is only the start. Getting your invention from the drawing board to market can take years of effort.

In some cases you may have to spend thousands of pounds of your own money on product development and promotional materials before a manufacturer will take interest.

For most inventors it's worth it, and there are certainly numerous cases of manufacturers offering millions for a single patent. By following our tips you too can follow in the footsteps of James Dyson and Ron Hickman and turn your brainchild into a multimillion pound earner.

Assistance And Information

The Patent Office, Cardiff Road, Newport, Gwent NP9 1RH Tel: 01633 813535.
http://www.patent.gov.uk
Will send free information on obtaining patents, copyrights and trademarks. Also offers counselling and unbiased advice, often for free.

Institute of Patentees and Inventors.
Tel: 020 7434 1818.
Offers its members advice on getting their invention to market. Also publishes books and holds inventors' meetings.

Chartered Institute of Patent Agents
Tel: 020 7405 945

CHAPTER 22

EARN HUGE COMMISSIONS AS A CONFERENCE BROKER

There's always an opportunity somewhere for helping buyers meet up with sellers, and taking a commission. Insurance broking is the most well known example, where brokers sell insurance policies on behalf of the insurance companies, earning substantial commissions in the process. Here's a service which could become equally as successful - conference broking. You can earn tens of thousands a year from finding conference clients on behalf of hotels.

Business is easy to find and you need no cash to get started - just organisational and interpersonal skills. Find out all about this winning opportunity.

Conferences Are Big Business

Large hotels make a great deal of money from hosting conferences. Firms will book a hotel's facilities to put on conferences, exhibitions, product launches, training seminars, dinner dances and other social events. This usually means booking accommodation, catering and technical equipment in addition to the actual conference room. Paying for these is not cheap, and the hotels do well out of it.

Most hotels, however, are lucky if they can get clients to use their conference facilities more than two days a week. Although this might be more than enough to justify the marketing expense - hosting conferences is highly lucrative remember - they end up with lots of spare capacity. Even the hotels that can afford to spend large amounts of money on marketing find that their resources are being spread thinly.

There's a way you can offer a solution to this problem. You can help companies market their services much more cheaply and efficiently, reduce their levels of spare capacity, improve their profitability and earn yourself big money in the process. How? By acting as a central conference organising agent on behalf of a number of hotels and conference venues in your area.

The idea is that you approach a number of hotels and offer to act as their conference broking agent. You find the client, book the venue and organise the conference on the client's behalf, and the hotels pay you for providing this service.

Increased Bookings And A Cheaper And Better Service

Why should hotels pay for a service they could provide themselves? Well, the hotels will benefit from increased bookings and reduced marketing costs. Imagine that in Anytown there are ten hotels paying, say, £5,000 a year each on marketing and promotion to find business clients to book their conference facilities - an annual total of £50,000. If they used your service, each one could contribute just £1,000 a year to the broking service's promotional budget, giving them a total of £10,000 a year to spend.

Instead of ten competing ads you need only place one, advertising a centralised conference organising service for Anytown on behalf of all ten hotels. However, instead of having £5,000 to spend on advertising and promotion you now have £10,000. With this money you can achieve a far wider advertising coverage and attract many more clients. So each hotel need only spend £1,000 a year on conference promotion, compared with the £5,000 they previously spent, and they are likely to get more bookings as a result.

There are benefits to clients too. When they want to book conference facilities they can speak to someone (you - the conference broker) with knowledge of all the conference venues in the area who can discuss their requirements in detail - the number of guests, accommodation, food, technical requirements and budget - and then book everything for them. You can save them the hassle of ringing round all the hotels themselves, you have in depth knowledge of the venues and so can find something to suit their requirements, and you can negotiate prices on their behalf.

Profits and Pay

Will a participating hotel lose potential bookings to other hotels using the service? No - because the conference agent books the hotels best suited to each client's needs and budget they are not prejudiced in any way, so the hotels don't lose out and the clients get a better service. However, there is scope for running the service as a co-operative and even sharing the profits between the hotels.

Although your clients will be companies, you will actually be paid by the hotels, most likely in the form of a commission payable on each booking. Alternatively, you could get hotels to club together to pay you a salary. Remember, if they have to employ one conference marketing person between them rather than one each, they will save money.

Setting up the Business

The way to set up a conference agency is to approach as many hotels as you can, explaining the features of the service, the advantages of using it, and the benefits it offers. Stress that you can help them get more bookings and reduce their marketing costs.

At the same time, do some market research on the demand for booking conferences. Send questionnaires to local companies asking whether they are likely to have any need to book conferences, and if so where, for how long, and for how many delegates. If you can prove to hotels that there is a demand they are more likely to use your conference broking service.

Finding Clients And Making Bookings

Pretty soon you should be able to start finding clients for the hotels that agree to use your service. Send information on your service directly to firms which may need to book conferences - especially large firms, and professional firms such as accountants and solicitors. Follow letters up with a phone call, with the purpose of setting up a personal visit. It is also worth advertising in the trade press, and in local newspapers and magazines.

Keep hotel brochures to show to clients and keep a database of all important information (the number of guests each hotel can accommodate, the size of its conference room, whether it provides audio-visual equipment, whether it offers catering and so on, plus prices).

Once you get an interested client, ascertain all their needs. You can make the booking for them, and confirm this in writing with both the hotel and the client. The client then pays the hotel for providing the facilities and (assuming you are not salaried) the hotel pays you commission for taking the booking.

Huge Commissions, Huge Scope for Expansion

If you are able to sell yourself you can make this service a huge success. There should be no trouble finding participating hotels, since you're offering them the chance to make more money at no risk to themselves. The clients get an improved service, and you get a whacking great commission. So everybody wins!

This service offers massive scope for expansion, since you needn't be restricted to one area. You could also attempt to attract individuals looking to book holidays and weekend breaks, therefore boosting your income potential.

Look around now for participating hotels and potential clients and start turning this lucrative business to your advantage.

CHAPTER
23

MAKE MONEY FROM MUSIC
Music Related Business Opportunities

The music business is one of the most lucrative and exciting industries to work in. It supports all kinds of people doing what they love, from singers, musicians and technicians through to people like CD sellers, music teachers and mobile DJs. If you are searching for a musical money spinner, look no further.

1.   Become A Mobile DJ

Spinning tunes for weddings and corporate bashes is a great business for anyone who likes to give others a good time. As a mobile DJ you will need a pair of record decks kitted out with a microphone and mixer, along with a powerful amplifier and set of speakers. Carry a sign featuring your name so that people will remember you. The key to your success will be your ability to tailor your records to the mood of the party. To cater for all tastes it is generally best to stick to crowd pleasers - 60s, 70s, 80s and current pop hits. It is a good idea to study other DJs - the music they play and how they interact with the crowd. Avoid the major error of playing the music *you* like - it is a total party wrecker.

You will soon develop your own style and as you discover how to get the crowds going, you can cater for larger events and charge even more. To market yourself, get business cards printed and leave them in shop windows, on notice boards in record shops, offices and so on, and advertise in the local paper and other entertainment related publications. It may be worth signing up with an entertainment agency. They'll take a cut from each booking, but they may be able to put a lot of work your way. Although it is a business where you work while others play, the best DJs become very well known and are never short of bookings.

2. Music Tuition

It is a sure-fire bet that any area of music you are skilled in, from playing a musical instrument through to home recording or DJ techniques, can be turned into profits. You could offer one-to-one classes in people's homes, or hire out a local community hall or even a recording studio to give classes for ten or more people at a time. Get bookings by handing out flyers, putting up posters, and by contacting organisations (e.g. schools, colleges, youth clubs, parent groups). Most importantly, get your pupils to recommend you to others.

Another option is to turn your skills into a range of teach yourself books, videos or cassettes, that could be sold via ads in music related publications and/or marketed through music shops. Alternatively, develop a mail order correspondence course. If you've no aptitude for music at all, pay experts to produce the course materials then make money from selling them.

3. CD Retail and Mail Order

If you're into music, then selling CDs, vinyl LPs and cassettes is a natural progression. In fact, buying and selling second-hand CDs is the ideal market stall business. Because they don't deteriorate you can pick up decent used stock very cheaply, and popular items will sell at a healthy mark up. You should either cater for a specialist area of music (jazz, classical, pop, or sixties music, for example) or stick to popular records that you know will sell. Encourage people to bring in CDs, which you can buy off them and resell at a profit.

Keep an eye out for record fairs in your area - they could provide a good source of income and stock for a record stall owner. Mail order is a profitable area, although it may work best if you target people with specialist musical interests. It is a good idea to run your operation on a club basis. Charge people an annual membership fee, give them a package of CDs (that you have purchased cheaply, of course) at the start of the year to entice them to join, and offer them your stock at a reduced rate. CD retail and mail order can be hugely profitable if you know the business well.

4.   Record Sourcing

Sourcing records - seeking out and buying specified records on behalf of a customer - is an area which many record enthusiasts and retailers are moving into. Many people collect old sixties singles, obscure jazz records, autographed records, imports and concert bootlegs for example, and might require particular items to complete their collection. They could contact someone to trawl the record shops and fairs on their behalf and collect a finder's fee when they have located the specified items. This is the ideal service if you're interested in snooping around racks of old records. Advertise it at record fairs, in record shops and in the music press.

5.   Buying and Selling Pop Memorabilia

It's not just the records people love - they'll pay big money for anything if it is related to a particular singer or band. Just look at the prices that Elvis and Beatles related memorabilia fetches at auctions all over the world. You could make money buying and selling memorabilia to collectors via ads in related publications, or buy things on their behalf in the same manner as a record sourcer, and collect a finder's fee.

6.   Live Performance

If you can play a musical instrument you can earn a crust providing background music at restaurants, pubs, bars, hotels and theatres, or even cruise ships. Check out the entertainment press, or try approaching places yourself. If you're a singer you could recruit a band (use small ads in the local paper or music press) or perform to backing tapes.

It is also well worth contacting local recording studios to see if they need singers or instrumentalists for session work. Remember, you don't have to aspire to selling out Wembley Arena - thousands of musicians make a solid living from working the pubs, working men's clubs or cruise ship circuit. If bookings are thin on the ground you can always take to busking.

7.   Fan Clubs

Behind any successful act you'll find a thriving fan club. Although most offer top quality service and products and provide a much demanded service for the fans, they are essentially exploiting a captive market and generate healthy profits as a result. Bearing this in mind, one possibility is to contact up and coming acts via their record companies and offer to run their fan club facility on a profit sharing basis. If they refuse, there's nothing stopping you running an unofficial fan club.

You'll need a computer with a database for storing personalised names and addresses. You will also need a word processor for producing a newsletter containing news, interviews and photographs of the person or group, along with letters from the fans, requests for pen pals, quizzes and puzzles, and so on. Don't forget to send out lists of merchandise. Many fan clubs organise functions and trips for members too. If you get involved just before an act takes off this could be a real money spinner.

8.   Song Writing

If you write a song which becomes successful the rewards can be amazingly high. Take "I Will Always Love You" by Whitney Houston. Every time it is played on the radio anywhere in the world, or is performed live - no matter who by - the songwriter collects a royalty payment. If you want to do the same, first you have to write, and copyright, your song. To get it recorded by a major artist and make some money you'll require a music publisher. These act as agents for songwriters and promote songs to record companies and artists, taking a percentage of the earnings, and they also help collect royalties from organisations such as the Performing Rights Society.

To earn a publishing contract you will need to send them a demo recording of yourself performing the song (most demo tapes contain two or three songs), along with a copy of the lyrics and a covering letter. A full list of publishers' addresses is available from the Music Publishers Association - Tel: 020 7839 7779. They may need to hear more before they make a decision, but if they like the songs enough they will offer you a publishing deal - at this point it is important to seek legal advice from a solicitor trained in the music business. If they can secure a recording of your song and it becomes a hit, they will collect performance and mechanical royalties on your behalf and will promote the song as widely as possible. For example, getting the song onto compilation albums, advertising jingles, films, TV and so on. If the publisher is doing its job it will still be promoting your song five, ten, even 15 years down the line. Remember, it might take just one hit song to set you up for life.

There is one tuly excellent course on how to succeed in the music business. It is called The Serious Writers Guild and it is run by Dec Cluskey. He knows this business inside out and back to front; I unreservedly recommend his course. Write to him at Stanton Prior, Darley Road, Meads, Eastbourne, BN20 7UH.

9.   Recording Songs and Music

Many songwriters hold the dream of attaining fame and fortune by performing their own songs, but there are all sorts of other ways to make money, depending on your skills. For example, you could offer a service writing and recording personalised songs - these might make excellent wedding, birthday or engagement gifts. Or, provide a service putting people's own lyrics to music. These could both be advertised in the entertainment section of the local paper as well as in the music press. Writing backing music for films, TV and computer games is another lucrative area. Approach these firms directly with samples of your work (if you have a publishing contract your publisher should do this for you). An alternative is to offer your music in copyright free form. In other words, the company gives you a one off payment for the music, which they can use in any way they want (as backing music for corporate videos or TV programmes for example) without having to worry about paying out royalties. The advantage to you is that you can still sell one piece of music many times over.

10.   Recording Sound and Special Effects

There is a big market for recordings of bird song, wildlife sounds, relaxing beach, sea, forest, river noises, railway sounds, and special effects that people can use for sound recordings, radio plays and so on. If you have suitable recording equipment, such as a portable minidisc recorder and microphone, you can very easily produce such tapes. Get 500 or 1000 made and sell them with ads in suitable publications, and/or get retailers to stock them.

11.   Musical Instrument Rental

Why not make money from renting out instruments such as drums, guitars, pianos and electronic keyboards, plus amplifiers, microphones, public address and sound recording equipment? Offer hourly, daily and weekly rates and promote the service to individuals, bands, schools and community groups. Provide deliveries too. You could advertise in the local paper and music press, and expand business by promoting the service in partnership with music shops. You could either handle the rental side of the business on their behalf (this would save you buying equipment), or get them to promote your service and take a cut on each booking.

12. Videos

These days every pop single released has to be accompanied by a promotional video for it to gain any kind of recognition. This means there are superb opportunities for aspiring video directors. If you've got the necessary ideas and equipment, try contacting record companies to see if they need anyone to make videos. It only takes one success to get your name known, at which point the sky will be the limit. Alternatively, if you only possess relatively basic equipment you could advertise in the music press to make cheap videos. The idea here is that you are making demo videos for bands to try and get a record deal. You can still charge £100-£200 for a day's work and make a very healthy living out of it.

13. Buying and Selling Musical Instruments

There is a ready market in the UK for unusual folk and ethnic instruments, so why not seek out a supplier and import them? Your local business library or Chamber of Commerce will carry trade directories from foreign countries. You can either distribute the instruments to retailers or sell them by mail order. An advantage is that the individuals and small firms overseas who make such products will be glad of any additional outlet, so prices (and your profit mark up) should be very reasonable.

14. Event Promotion

Promoting concerts can be a great way to get a profitable foothold in the entertainment business. The principle is the same whether you put on rock gigs in your local pub or choral concerts in the community hall. First, you need to book the act(s) and the venue, ensuring that there are adequate facilities for the entertainers and the audience. You need to promote the event widely - put up plenty of posters, hand out flyers, leave piles of leaflets in pubs, bars, shops, theatres and so on, send press releases to the local media, plus free tickets to get reviews, and have competitions and ticket give-aways in the local press - these methods all help to get publicity. You must sell tickets too - the venue will usually have its own box office, or at least will sell tickets for you, and you could sell them in other outlets such as record shops or tourist information centres.

It is a good idea to set up a telephone line to deal with reservation credit card bookings. Finally, you must co-ordinate proceedings at the event itself. You may have to hire extra front of house security and backstage staff. When you are planning the event, put together a budget and keep in mind the number of tickets you need to sell to break even. That way you will always know how hard you have to work to hit that figure.

15. Entertainment Agency

Being an agent is a wonderful job for anyone who loves talking to people. An agent signs up artists and takes a commission whenever they can get them work. This means believing in the artists and working for them 100%. The best agents cultivate a wide network of contacts and are able to use them to secure bookings. You will need to advertise in all kinds of entertainment related publications in the early days, both for new clients and bookings, although as you build up a solid and successful client roster, the bulk of your business will be conducted on the phone.

16. Musical Trips

Many of the world's biggest musical acts tend to only play a handful of stadium dates in the UK in places like Wembley Arena and Birmingham NEC, as opposed to playing smaller venues all over the country. This makes it difficult for all the fans to see a particular act, but means there's a growing demand for coach trips to rock and pop concerts. You could offer a travel only ticket or provide a concert ticket and coach package deal - adding a decent mark up of course. To maximise your income you could also provide musical sightseeing tours.

17.   Hiring Out Studio Space

Bands need somewhere to rehearse, so if you've got an old garage or a spare part of an office you can earn money by leasing it out as a practice room. All it needs is to be reasonably soundproof and have a few power points and a heater for when it's cold. You could get two or three bands to share the rehearsal room and pay according to the number of hours they use it, or one band could pay a retainer to have the room exclusively. Whatever, you will probably only need to put up a few postcards in the early days. Once you've got some regular bookings you can sit back and rake in the cash.

18.   Be a Roadie

If you've got absolutely no musical talent but don't mind lugging heavy equipment, then being a roadie could be the perfect job for you. It can be fairly well paid if you are working for a name act who tour regularly, but you'll need to be prepared to put up with cramped, hot and often very loud working (and travelling) conditions, and generally being the lowest of the low. Aside from the wages, the compensations are that it can be extremely good fun. You might get to mix with some talented and well known musicians, and if you're very lucky, with the fans too! The best way to get work is to approach bands directly - at gigs, for example - and to put up postcards at recording studios and practice rooms.

CHAPTER 24

Classic Car Garage

Classic Car enthusiasts will travel miles and willingly go off the beaten track to visit a classic car garage. If you don't own a property with a large enough piece of land or a spare building, farms often have spare barns available for renting. With a little bit of work and imagination, a barn can be turned into a really exciting Classic Car Garage.

Fitting Out the Garage

You can really go to town on the décor for a classic car garage. Buying up a few old cars that are not worth doing up, can reap a treasure of bits and pieces: headlights, bumpers, arm indicators, steering wheels, hub caps, door handles, radiator grilles, car manufacture emblems. Collect some pictures of classic cars, old racing pictures with the racing drivers standing by their car.

If you can't find pictures any other way, simply buy magazines, cut out the pictures and mount them yourself. Decide on what frames to use and once chosen use all the same style for a neater display. With a bit of imagination a few pots of paint, some shelving and helpful workers from the family, you can turn your garage from a desolate barn to an interesting environment full of 'talking pieces' to captivate your customers as soon as they walk through the doors.

Remember the old design for all the harvesters restaurants? They had bits of ploughs and old farm tools hanging from the ceilings, wrapped round beams etc. The walls were also covered with prints in frames of old farm workers pulling ploughs, holding onto the horse's bridle etc. You can use the same technique in a garage.

The floor will be the showroom space for the classic cars for sale. I have been to several classic car garages where the floor is earth and it really didn't matter. So, if the floor of the building you're using is earth, it's fine. As with any new enterprise, it's a great help if you can find ways of looking prosperous to attract your customers, without spending a fortune, in fact search for cheap ways to design your garage.

The Selling Technique

The most exciting part of selling classic cars is that everyone who visits your garage, is not simply looking for the family saloon, but for a car they can love and cherish. This is very important when it comes to the selling techniques.

First and foremost, most of your clients will be relaxed and friendly as soon as they discover that you are passionate about the vehicles you have for sale. If you adopt the attitude that rather than trying to sell, you're merely showing off your cars to a friend, then your sales spiel won't sound like sales talk.

Invite customers' to touch the bodywork and run their hands over the splendid huge curve of an Austin Princess's boot. Invite them to sit in the driver's seat and enjoy the leather seats, run their hands over the mahogany dashboards. If you can do all these things in an enticing way, you're obvious love for these old vehicles will inspire the confidence in your clients to allow their enthusiasm to show.

The Psychology Behind Buying Classic Cars

Understanding some of the reasons why classic cars are sought after, can be an enormous help in selling them.

For most people the main reason they want a classic car is simply it's like a trip down memory lane. Often a car is a desired object of their teenager years. Someone who was dating girls and living the bachelor life in the 60's is likely to be interested in any of the classics, from a Ford Anglia to one of the Triumph sports cars – depending on what they owned in their teens. If they were from an upper middle class family, the classic car that would be of interest is more likely to be from a Rover to an Austin Healey.

Most men have a bit of James Bond in them and because of this the classic sports cars are always very popular. For this reason, some garages only specialise in sports cars and often even sports cars of one make.

A high proportion of women will often accompany their husbands to help with the choice or purchase a car for themselves.

Buying Stock

Some car auctions have special days set aside for classic cars. Example: Blackbushe car auctions in Hampshire.

Apart from looking out for good private purchases, motoring clubs run adverts from their members in their monthly magazines or newsletters. These are excellent places to advertise. Most of these clubs only cost about £25 to join for the entire year and for that sometimes the advertising is free or at the very least nominal to members.

Joining these clubs will put you in touch with:
Enthusiasts,

suppliers of classic car parts.
Insurance companies for classic cars
and give Classic Car Show dates.

These magazines and newsletters will expand your ideas
on other services you can offer to your customers. For example:
you can put them in touch with specialist insurance companies.
First-time purchasers of classic cars don't realise that
photographs are needed for the insurance company before they
can insure the vehicle. Here's a service you can offer buyers.
All you need is a Polaroid camera.

Advertising

A visit to newsagents will furnish you with a pile of classic
car newspapers and magazines. All you need at first is to place
an advert for one of your cars and explain a classic car garage
with stock. And of course, probably the best place of all is the
club magazines and newsletters.   Any of these will also be open
to accepting editorial items from you. Although there will be no
pay, the returns from free advertising will more than
compensate.

CHAPTER 25

Antique Clocks

If you like collectibles and want to specialise in a high demand area, then selling antique clocks is worth considering. Again with a little imagination, this can be a great business.

The premises

Here's an unusual idea for the premises, one that can work very well. On a visit to a large house on a private estate, I was surprised to discover a wing had been rented out to a large blue-chip insurance company. But, what interested me more when I was shown round, was the furniture; every piece was for sale. Each item of antique furniture had a white ticket hanging from a piece of string, with the price marked.

I discovered, that a local antique dealer had struck an agreement with the owner of the house and the insurance company, to be allowed to display the furniture in return for a share of the profit from sales.

This arrangement benefited the insurance company, because they didn't need to buy furniture for the huge reception area. The antique dealer had ready-made clients coming through the doors on a regular basis throughout each day, namely the insurance company's clients. These people all had one very important thing in common for the antique dealer; they were all wealthy. His furniture was displayed in a grand setting at no cost to him, until he made a sale. He simply had to add a small percentage to the profit margin to cover their cut.

If you can hunt down a company not too far away from you, with the same type of scenario, you could display your clocks. Large houses open to the public, could be another venue. All you have to do is to make the proposal.

Other clocks can also be displayed in a spare building in your garden or a spare room in your own house – again imagination will turn it into something unique and special.

Advertising

Advertise in magazines like Country Life and the BBC Home and Antiques. They also carry advertising for clock restorers and repairers. However, if you do use a clock restorer, make sure you tie them down to a specific time to complete the repairs; it can take 6 months to get a clock back.

Dates of Antique fairs are also advertised in the BBC Antiques magazine and Country Life.

CHAPTER 26

Teddy Bear Hospital

One of the most endearing of all toys is the teddy bear. And according to a toy bear expert, men tend to be much more sentimental about their bears than women!

The first bear was made by an American toy-maker in 1902, to commemorate an act of mercy by the president, which captured the nation's imagination. Despite being a keen hunter, President Theodore Roosevelt, spared the life of an orphaned bear. So the very first bear was named after the president's nickname, 'Teddy'. Ever since the furry toys have been called teddy bears.

Because they are so popular, many teddy bears are kept by their owners' way past childhood. Of course this means that many bears need to be repaired at some point. They tend to lose an eye, or an arm comes unstitched, or they may lose a paw pad. Some fall victims to an attack by a pet dog or they can suffer from carpet beatles which eat the fur.

Older bears are usually stuffed with kapok or woodwool, while modern toys are mostly filled with synthetic materials. Some types of man-made stuffing disintegrates into a soggy mess which sinks to the bottom of the bear's legs.

Making Repairs

To learn the trade, The Encyclopaedia of Teddy Bears lists bears past and present. Many of the older bears are rare and valuable. To repair bears requires a mixture of sewing and embroidery skills. Sometimes a bear's face has to be constructed from just a chewed up hole. The expression of the renewed face has to be the same as before the dog got to the bear. Photographs in the Encyclopaedia give you a picture to work from.

Marketing

Build a portfolio of before and after pictures of bears. They can be mounted on the walls of the hospital alongside any 'thank you' letters from owners of repaired bears. Also, encourage owners to let you take a photograph of their daughter or son clutching their newly repaired teddy bear. Such photographs are very appealing and instil confidence in new customers of your capabilities and care for the bears.

Work out a sheet of 'Caring for your Teddy Bear' and type the list out for customers, which you give to them free.

The 'hospital' could be in a workroom behind a shop selling teddy bears, which either belongs to you or to another company.

Advertising

Choose the toy and collector magazines. Offer an alternative to visiting; posting bears for repair work.

Teddy bears are very emotive and this should be reflected in your advertising strategy.

Further Information

The Teddy Bear Museum, 19 Greenhill, Stratford-upon-Avon. Tel: 01789 293160. It is open daily from 9.30am to 6pm, except 25th and 26th December.

Broadway Dolls and Bears, 76 High Street, Broadway, Worcestershire. Tel: 01386 858323. Open Tuesday to Sunday, from 10am to 5pm.

CHAPTER 27

How to Make Money from Organising Collector's Fairs

You could merely hire out local halls and advertise the venues and dates in local papers. However, by initiating unusual marketing techniques, success and profits can be increased at least ten-fold if not more. So, even if you don't find organising collector's fairs an appealing idea, the following thought-provoking ideas can be used to increase profits in many other businesses.

The Success Strategy

Going the extra mile increases profits and fun. First on the agenda: if you are contemplating organising collector's fairs as a source of income, make sure it's something you would like to do. If you enjoy hunting out old treasures yourself, or think spending a Saturday afternoon at a collector's fair is fun, you'll have the built in enthusiasm and drive to succeed.

Next, choose a strong business name and create a memorable image by using a logo. The name and logo should reflect the business. For example: (name) Collector's Fairs, say, Wilson's Collector's Fairs, or Joe's Collector's & Memorabilia Fairs. Decide whether you wish to appeal to upmarket buyers or the mass market.

Ask the vital question, who are my clients? If you want to attract the mass market, then you go downmarket. A prime example of this in fashion is the Joe Bloggs label – the name appeals to many, so the profits are phenomenal.

If only the wealthier clients appeal to you, then your business name will be upmarket. Examples of this in the antiques world of course, are Christie's and Sothebys. The 'auction house' part of Sothebys and Christie's, is almost superfluous to the names, and delegated to second place. With both of those auction houses, we all know the goods are quality and expensive.

If you choose this route, then looking at our example, Wilson's would be in large letters and Collector's Fairs would be in small, and it might even be positioned on all stationery away from the main business name. The mass market option, can be splashed exuberantly across all of the stationery.

Stationery

That's the next step, have your business stationery printed. Items you'll need:
letterheads – not just for writing letters, but so you can open a bank account for your business –
compliment slips – very useful for enclosing with brochures you post out –
business cards – drum up business by leaving a pile on the entrance table, at every fair you organise –
invoices – have the two page pads printed up, it's easy to tear off top copy and give to the stall holders leaving the base copy for your own files.

Advertising Strategy

Your advertising will reflect the choice of upmarket or mass market. Let's take upmarket choice first. Consider advertising in the classifieds at the back of Country Life magazine. After a few successful venues approach the editorial staff of Country Life, with a view to seeing if they would be interested in a short article accompanied by a photograph.

For mass market, the advertising place would be the local newspaper to the area you have organised a venue. Local magazines and papers should be interested in running editorial. They are more likely to agree if you provide them with a ready made editorial piece accompanied by a photograph.

It's possible to lift your advertising from the mundane, by putting in a few well chosen words that highlight how anyone can pay a few £'s for 'tat' to discover it's a treasure worth a fortune! Note: the word 'tat' is only fine to use for the mass market, the upmarket clientele would probably be offended. Alternative word of course, is junk. Or, 'Grandmother's Old Treasures' is a phrase that conjures images and emotions of 'memories of the past'. Powerful emotive marketing! Both of the latter suggestions are suitable for mass or upmarket advertising.

Leaflets and Brochures

It's much easier to create powerful marketing through an A5 leaflet or small brochures, than an advertisement in a newspaper or magazine, simply because you have much more room to say your piece. (In the marketing section we'll be looking at designs and ideas behind successful selling through leaflets and brochures and how to produce them.)

Distribute the leaflets and brochures by:
handing them out to shoppers in towns,
pinning them up on the boards in newsagents and local stores in villages – charges are often only 50p a week,
asking local service businesses to display a small pile for visitors to pick up. Examples: – solicitors, estate agents, health centres, local libraries (depends on individuals working in these places whether they agree or not).

How to Contact Sellers of Collectibles

As with any new business, one of the very first priorities is to build a substantial client base. With organising collector's fairs you have two sets of clients – sellers and buyers – and you have to find both. As long as the leaflets, brochures and adverts have invitation for sellers to contact you then that will attract a number of sellers.

But it should pay dividends, if you visited memorabilia and collector's fairs and shops, junk and antique shops and fairs, attended craft fairs, handing a brochure or leaflet to each of the traders. Once you build a reputation for running well-organised successful collector's fairs, traders will travel the length and breadth of the country to attend.

Create Extra Interest

Always carry a camera around with you, at each venue. Take photographs that you think can be used for articles in magazines, newspapers, adverts, for a web site and for your brochures and leaflets.

Also consider taking video. TV production companies are always on the lookout for 'off the wall' docu soaps. If you shoot just a small amount of interesting enough film you could convince a production team to make an entire docu soap about you and your business, which would be free advertising. By the way, don't expect payment from the production company, they don't pay, but consider the free air time you'll get, more than fair recompense – and they're right.

Here's another strategy for increasing the interest in collecting. Type 'lucky find stories' onto A4 sheets and insert into photograph stands, and place these around each venue, where visitors will read them. You are more than welcome to use any of the true stories on pages 10 – 14 of this issue, word for word.

There are many 'collecting' interest magazines, on sale in newsagents. What better place to sell these than at your

138

Collector's Fairs? Even if the profit margins from selling the magazines are low, it will increase your overall profits, because it is another strategy that will set your venues apart from others.

Call the magazine publishers direct, explain your business and find out if they are willing to post you a small number at discount price. Check to see if they are also willing to offload out of date issues at next to nothing or even free, with the understanding you charge a nominal sum for them at your collector's fairs. Your criteria is to increase the number of 'collecting' enthusiasts, thereby increasing the number of people who attend all your venues.

On the same table, you could also sell books on the subject.

Album of Treasure Finds

Over time, build a photograph album of interesting finds, and leave this album open on a table for people to look at.

To create the articles, you'll need to have forms printed which start with a quick and punchy letter from yourself. The letter would begin with a story of a fantastic find, (again, if you wish you can use any of the true stories from pages 10 – 14, word for word with our permission) followed by an invitation for people to tell you about their lucky treasure finds.

Even some of the stall holders could be willing to show-off a prize picked up for a few pence at a car boot sale, which they know is worth £500. If you find the take-up on this slow, simply initiate a competition – offering the writer of the best lucky treasure find story, a cash, collector's piece or book token prize.

Choosing the Venues

This will depend on how much travelling you want to do. Collector's Fairs are mostly run on Saturday and sometimes Sundays. Because they're only once a week affairs, it gives you plenty of time for the administration side of the business – finding suitable venues and working out the advertising strategy.

Possible venues are: School halls – hiring rates can range from £5 to £12 an hour – depending on the area – Berkshire is expensive, while Cumbria is cheap.
Village halls - these are usually cheaper – ranging from £3 to £8 an hour.
Old Town halls – some older towns have beautiful listed buildings that they no longer use as the town hall, but hire out for functions – the price depends on the local council.
Hotels – probably the dearest option - but it depends on your business, if it's upmarket then hotels could be the place.

Check the chosen venues are well lit and have ample electricity points. Also make sure there is a supply of chairs and tables.

Make sure there is plenty of car parking space, for both sellers (who also need to know they don't have to walk half a mile with armfuls of collectibles) and buyers.   Also check you're allowed to put up signs locally, advertising the venue to attract passers by.

Booking in the Sellers

Design a booking form, which contains requests of the following information: Name, address, telephone number and email, how many tables are required (charge per table), tables or chairs required, electricity requirements.

Collect the money before the venue. If you're a new business, you may have to start with collecting 50% deposit, not refunded if they don't turn up, and the remaining 50% payable on the day.

How much you charge per table will depend on the cost of a venue. Charges have to be made in line with the local economy, so, it's essential to research each area.

Using the Internet

Once the business takes off there is no reason why you shouldn't create a website for your business. It can be as simple or complete as you wish, even downloading a brochure for surfers to browse through. Bookings could be taken over the Internet if you set it up with credit card payment facilities.

The cost of someone else designing a website for you, can range from £1,000 upwards, so it's not cheap. But if your business is taking off in leaps and bounds, the extra trade could catapult your collector's fairs into big time and big money.

We all love a bargain! So why not turn this love into a fun way of earning your livelihood?

Extra information:
Auction Houses
Christie's - 020 7581 7611
Sothebys – 020 7493 8080
Bonhams – 020 7393 3939

Dealers/Specialists
Vintage Magazine Company 020 7439 8525
British Antiques Dealers' Association – 020 7589 4128

Further Reading
The Which? Guide to Buying Antiques (which? Monthly)
A Fortune in Your Attic – Tony Curtis (Lyle Publications)
Miller's Collectibles Price Guide (Reeds Consumer Books)
The Successful Investor – Robin Duthy (Collins)
Enclyclopaedia of Everyday Antiques (David & Charles)

WH Smith stock magazines covering collectibles, memorabilia and antiques. All worth buying.

CHAPTER 28

Producing Powerful Marketing Literature

With any new business, keeping costs low in the early days is critical. However, it's just as critical to launch under the banner of strong advertising. With today's technology it's easy.

Basic Requirements

You need a computer and printer – not necessarily a colour printer. Although they are still very cheap to buy, the paper and printing costs (cartridges) are higher. Ink jet printers are cheaper than laser, but bear in mind the ink can come off if your leaflets or brochures get wet. You don't need to be a touch typist, or designer, just have some patience and the willingness to learn. If you already own a computer with Microsoft Word or any other word packaging, you will have all you need to design all of your own marketing literature if you decide to.

There will be time later on for you to buy a more sophisticated design programme, like photoshop if the idea appeals, but it's certainly not essential.

Designer Stationery

Office suppliers such as Viking Direct, provide a wide range of papers for you to print on. Designer papers are A4 sheets with coloured images already printed, ready for your own text to be printed onto. Here's a list of designs, to give you an idea of the fantastic range: Pretty pansies, playful teddies, orcas, sunset, paper tulips, candles, wooded path, horizon, daisy garden, first kiss, imperial, books, Stonehenge, dolphins, polar bears, saddle, whales, penguins, waves, teddy bears, marina, golf course, coffee house, tech, fall harvest, party, beach, scroll, sunflower, eagle, leaping salmon, clouds, sunflowers, music, surf, grey, green and sand marble, butterfly, rainbow, hot news, gala, stop press, dove, watercolour border.

As you can appreciate from the list, there is a paper suitable for many businesses. If you're opening a golf club, then consider the golf course designer paper for your letterheads. For anyone starting up a holiday homes business, there are several choices: orcas, sunset, paper tulips, wooded path, horizon, Stonehenge, dolphins, waves, marina, golf course, beach, rainbow. For opening a cafe, there's the coffee shop paper.

If you need a more sophisticated paper for your business or company, the marble and imperial papers are impressive and very upmarket. The cost (through Viking Direct) is usually £4.99 per pack of 100 sheets. That's all you may need to start up in business; merely one pack of 100 pages. Print out your business or company name and details and you have all you need to open a bank account and for writing letters to clients.

There are also pages of card you can put through printers, to print out your own business cards. For compliment slips, merely, design three to one A4 page and cut with a scalpel (two cuts per page to produce each batch of three compliment slips).

Special Promotions

The Stop Press and Hot News sheets, can be used for any special promotions. Simply type out what you want to say and print onto the pages. Unfortunately, I don't think any company produces these marvellous designer papers on A5 size sheets, so that they could be used for small leaflets. So, these pages are only suitable for letterheads or A4 promotional leaflets.

Brochures

It's a simple matter to design your own brochures with the specially designed brochure pages available. After printing your text onto the A4 pages they simply have to be folded into three. The backgrounds are designed to make the folding easy and the end result is a cheap in-house produced brochure that looks professional.

Laminating

Another relatively cheap method of producing marketing literature in-house, is to purchase a laminating machine. They cost approx. £90 +VAT. It can be useful to laminate any leaflets you want to display for long term, especially if clients are going to be picking them up to read, or they are displayed outdoors. Lamination is a process which bonds a thin sheet of clear plastic to the surface of the printed page, giving it a durable shiny finish.

The Copy

How do you write powerful copy (words which will sell your product), if you are not a copywriter?

Here are some basic guidelines:
Communicate directly to your readers, by writing as if you were talking to them. Correct grammar is not the most important issue – being understood is.

Don't be frightened to use large headings that are witty and eye-catching – newspapers and magazines make good research places for getting to grips with powerful headings.

Grab Your Readers' Attention

In the very first sentence! If you don't you may lose them. We live at a fast pace. Concentration is not high on our priority list. Just look at the designs of many of the popular magazines and you can see that short, snappy articles, interlaced with plenty of pictures, are the normal layout. Pick up any Dorling Kindersley book and see how they have revolutionised learning from books with their layouts.

Make what you have to say exciting and interesting.

Word Choices

Choose your words carefully. Be aware of the sound words make. For instance, let's suppose you want to inject some humour into your text, certain words are funnier than others. An example of this is one of Beryl Reid's lines when she was doing a routine, knocking her girlfriend, Deirdre. She'd say, 'Deirdre says her complexion is sallow…I call it yellow…what with her yellow face and her little black eyes, she looks like a small portion of prunes and custard!'

This dialogue wouldn't have half the punch if Beryl had chosen to use apricots and custard, instead of prunes and custard, because prunes is a funny word and apricots isn't.

Another classic technique for working out a punch line is to use alliteration. Example: I bet he's bonking some bimbo in the back seat!' (Much funnier than, 'I'm certain he's having sex with some girl in the rear of the car.' It means the same, but it certainly does not have the same impact.)

So if you're stuck for a powerful headline or a business/company motto, then try alliteration.

Emotive Text

Stories or headings that appeal to our emotions and trigger fond memories, are powerful selling allies. For many people, life today is too stressful. We are bombarded from all sides, with calls on our mobiles at any time of day or night, emails to check, forms to fill in and too many rules to live by imposed on us by unworkable politics. Any references to (say) the 60's, conjures up images of much simpler, relaxed fun-filled days. It's not important that the era was not perfect - no era is - or that they didn't reap the benefits of the incredible technology of mobiles or the Internet.

Text which is geared towards family life, is also a powerful marketing tool, simply because the world can be a very frightening place, and the throwaway society (which includes throwing away relationships) is taking a swing towards a desire for more stability through lasting relationships.

The Reason for Copywriting

The only reason you're creating strong headlines and text is to sell a service, your ideas or products. So, if you want to write great copy, make sure it will produce the desired result of increased profit. Decide on the mood and pace that will initiate the highest sales in your particular marketplace.

If you have no desire to write your own copy, then there is the option of employing a copywriter on a freelance basis as and when you need copy basis, or a marketing person as an employee.

Extra Information

Viking Direct Office Supplier: Freephone on 0800 424444

CHAPTER 29

Ayurvedic Businesses

The number of people incorporating holistic systems into their lifestyle increases daily, making Ayurveda a growing business for anyone interested in herbal and holistic medicines. The facts at the start are to give you some background text for sales literature. It can be used word for word if you wish.

What is Ayurveda?

Ayur means life and Veda stands for knowledge or science. Both are Sanskrit words and their meanings reveal that Ayurveda is a holistic system of healing based on the interaction of body, mind and spirit.

Thought to be the oldest health care system in the world, it originated from the Himalayas over 5000 years ago. Prophets and Rishis passed on their wisdom by reciting the system from teacher to disciple and eventually it was all set down in Sanskrit poetry known as the Vedas.

The Vedas were written down in approximately 1500 BC and form the basis of the Indian culture.

The Principles of Ayurveda

The system teaches a belief that everything in the universe is made up of five elements. This includes the human body. The five elements are: ether, air, fire, water and earth. Each of these elements are composed of three bio-energies known as doshas and they influence all our mental and physical processes.

The air principle, VATA, is created from ether and air. The fire principle, PITTA, is the product of fire and water. The water principle, KAPHA, is produced from earth and water.

Ayurveda is about balancing these five elements and the doshas for perfect health of mind, body and spirit. According to the system, we are all born with a particular balance of Vata, Pitta and Kapha. There is always a dominant dosha in each of us and this dictates our body type, temperament and susceptibility to illness.

Prakruti is the basic constitution, which remains unaltered throughout our lives.

The way to perfect health is to keep our doshas in a state of personal balance. If this balance is disturbed through foods, lifestyle or emotional problems, it erupts into physical discomfort, pain, or mental illness. Negative emotions such as fear and jealousy can take over our lives creating further anxiety and the state of imbalance that can cause such symptoms to occur is known as Vikruti.

Ayurvedic Healing

Ayurveda is a system for healthy living. Depending on your own personal balance of doshas, you can regain and maintain perfect mind and body health, simply by knowing which foods suit you, whether they are better hot or cold, raw or cooked.

To remedy imbalances of the doshas, herbal medicines are also used. They are chosen for each individual to balance their doshas. For example: an excess of Kapha could cause, lethargy, fluid retention, overweight and catarrh. The treatment would consist of a diet of warm, light dry foods with care to avoid wheat, milk products and sugar which all increase Kapha.

Herbs would also be prescribed. They would include warming spices like cinnamon, pepper, cloves and ginger to increase the circulation, digestive fire and cleanse toxins from the body.

The choice of herbs are based on quality or energy which Ayurveda determines according to 20 attributes such as hot, cold, wet, dry, heavy or light. They are also classified according to the six tastes of sweet, sour, salty, pungent, bitter and astringent.

- Kapha is increased by sweet, sour and salty foods – which also decrease Vata.
- Vata is increased by pungent, bitter and astringent foods – which also decrease Kapha.
- Pitta is increased by pungent, sour and salty foods.
- Sweet, bitter and astringent foods decrease Pitta.

Ayurvedic Practitioner

If the subject really interests you, then you may wish to study to become an Ayurvedic Practitioner. They assess Prakruti and Vikruti, to form an opinion of your basic constitution and your current state of health.

This is what it involves: Taking a detailed case history and examining the body.
Assessing the body build, condition of the skin and hair type, body temperature, digestion and bowel function.

When the individual's doshic balance and the causes of the imbalance has been assessed, treatment and lifestyle advice is given.

Obviously to enter this business, you need training. For information of places you can train, a supplier of Ayurvedic products is: The Ayurvedic Shop, 299 King Street, Hammersmith, London W6 9NH. Their website: www.the-ayurvedic-shop.co.uk.

Selling Ayurvedic Products

Books, the herbal remedies, magazines and all Ayurvedic related products can be sold either in a shop or by direct mail.

Training Courses

Another opportunity is once you have learned the art and earned the necessary qualification certificates, you can train other people to be practitioners.

Other opportunities in the training area, are:
Lectures on Ayurveda
Yoga classes
Ayurvedic massage.

Ayurvedic & Beauty

Opening a Beauty Parlour, you could offer relaxing Ayurvedic massage and Indian head massage, followed by a make-up session of natural beauty products.

Research Source

The main book for studying the system in depth, is the Charaka Samhita. They are the writings of a scholar who lived and taught around 700 BC, that are still considered to be the main authority of Ayurveda and are referred to constantly by practitioners of today.

CHAPTER 30

Home Search Service

Searching for the perfect home is time consuming and costly. So many people are just far too busy to spare the time for house searching and so it's a good business to set up.

Setting Up

All you need is an office, telephone, a computer and to be linked to the Internet. Decide on a business name, which may depend on whether you decide to set up a nationwide home search or an area (e.g. Sussex) home search. Check the classifieds in magazines like Country Life, Home and Gardens for businesses already in existence so that you don't repeat an area already well covered by other search companies.

After placing some adverts, design forms asking for each client's requirements. You'll need to know:
Name and Address details plus contact numbers.
Location required: rural, semi-rural or town or specific place.
Number of rooms required.
Garden size.
Is a garage important?
Any special requirements, e.g. conservatory.

Prefer old or new houses?
Terrace, Semi-detached or detached?
Flat, apartment, bungalow or house?
Do you want to rent or buy?

With a good laser printer you can print your own professional looking forms and post them out when new clients contact you.

Searching for Properties

Your research places are: magazines, the Internet, building societies.

To find out what to charge, a little research will reveal what other search companies charge.

Overseas Home Search Service

Many people retire to warmer climes but often want their property all sorted out before they actually retire. If you have a language then this is an added advantage in the service you can offer to people wanting to purchase in a foreign country – even a predominantly English speaking country. A person who can speak Spanish, for instance, will know if the price quoted for a property is in line with the country's house prices. It can be easier to study a country's economic situation if you speak the language. However, it's not vital.

Legal Issues

A service for Home Search in another country can extend into other services. For instance, the legal issues of house-buying alter between countries. You can make sure your clients don't get caught out. In Spain, if you buy a house from people who have debts on the house, you become legally bound to pay their debts. In other countries houses have been built without planning permission.

In Turkey, you have to pay £30,000 (which you can use for buying a house) into a bank account before you are eligible to buy a property in the country.

So, whichever country you decide to home search, you need to study the quirks of the house buying system and find a good lawyer in that country for your clients.

Extra Services

Once a property has been found and purchased, there are other services which some overseas clients would appreciate. They are:
- Sorting out repairs or building work (their fee depending on how much time you have to spend booking and chasing up builders)
- Interior Design (can even include all linen and kitchen utensils)
- Decorating
- Sorting out the garden

Of course, all of these extra services can apply to properties found at home as much as abroad.

Business Property Searchers

When businesses and companies, large or small want to move to a different area they don't always wish to use a managerial staff member to search for new offices, factories or shop premises.

Some clients who want to purchase (as opposed to renting or leasing) may even be happy for you to attend property sales on their behalf – especially if they want to keep the potential office move secret from their competitors or shareholders. This is how it works: once the bidding starts on a property they're interested in, you bid, keeping in contact with your client by mobile. You simply tell them the price the bid stands at and they direct your next bid.

The approach for obtaining business clients is a blend of visiting companies and advertising in business magazines. You could also send a pamphlet of your services to all the Business Development and Business Support agencies in the areas your business covers (banks also support these local enterprise agencies). Contacting your local Borough Council should reveal a source of the business agencies.

CHAPTER 31

Grave Tending Service

It is always sad when a loved one dies, although one of the things that can console us after their passing is the thought that their graveside is being looked after.

But tending a grave or memorial plot is not always as easy as it sounds. Due to personal preferences and logistical factors, relatives, friends and loved ones are not always buried as close to us as we would wish. Subsequently, the distances involved, the possible time and expense incurred, and many cases a lack of transport facilities all mean that we are not able to look after the graveside as much as we would like.

A business that offers people a chance to do something about this widespread problem is the grave tending service. It has become an established service in the USA and, far from being morbid, it is a caring people-friendly business that can be set up and run very easily. For an equivalent of £5 - £10 per month your employees would clean up the gravestones and plot, clearing out any old flowers and replacing them with new ones.

Advertising your service

Take out newspaper ads. Try placing an ad. in the same section as funeral services and distribute business cards and leaflets. This should result in a solid client base. Running an agency, you can offer the service for the entire country or choose an area e.g. Midlands.

The aim is to run a community-friendly service that offers your employees a full or part time income.

CHAPTER 32

A Bodyguard Agency

In this day and age bodyguards are big business and can command huge daily rates. But is the demand there, and can the average bodyguard earn a decent crust?

The answer is emphatically yes on both counts. More people than ever before are commissioning bodyguards for a great variety of tasks, and there are excellent business opportunities in all areas.

Bodyguards are much more than security men and don't just protect celebrities. They are often used by businesses to escort wage collections, by banks to stand outside cash point machines and deter undesirables, or by individuals as escorts. Sometimes they are used to carry cash and valuables and are even hired by businessmen to accompany them on business trips.

Employees

Setting up an agency, you would advertise for bodyguards to join, who are very adaptable, as well as big and strong, reliable and discreet. Your employees should be prepared to undertake any job the client requires (within reason), and be prepared to work at any time. Occasionally the work can be glamorous, say if they were working for a celebrity or as a personal escort, but they need to be prepared for anything.

Charges to hire a bodyguard vary depending on the client, the work and the bodyguard's experience. But on average you should expect to charge £200 a day.

Bodyguards and their agents tend not to advertise as such, other than in the Yellow Pages, Thomson Directory and similar, but you could advertise in local newspapers and hand out business cards to prospective clients just to get the agency started. Your main form of advertising will be from the recommendations of satisfied customers, so make sure each customer is happy with the agency's service. This should result in repeat business from permanent contracts.

A varied, enjoyable and potentially lucrative business, running a bodyguard agency could be the key to your future security.

CHAPTER 33

The Helping Hands Agency

People who work long hours, or have to juggle work commitments with looking after a family, have very busy lives.

Most of us grudgingly put up with tasks like cleaning, cooking, shopping and washing. Well paid professionals who work long hours, on the other hand, are less likely to be bothered with such things, but have the advantage of being able to pay money for other people to do their chores.

There's a great opportunity for someone to set up an agency taking care of all kinds of household tasks, from the aforementioned chores to things like decorating, picking up children, walking dogs and doing the gardening, or anything else required by clients.

Such work would be ideal for any handy person, and would make an excellent part or full time business for a retired person who wants to earn some extra cash, or a housewife or husband with some free time to spare. These are benefits that will attract employees to your agency. By targeting well off areas, the agency would soon be up and running.

Extra Business

But this is only half the story. Anyone who really wants to make a mint from this agency should look towards business as well as personal clients. Take estate agents - they need the homes they are selling to look as good as possible, so you could approach them to help spruce up their houses - cleaning, redecorating, even freshening the place up and putting out fresh flowers. Building contractors may require similar work, and your agency may even be called upon to choose, buy and install furniture, fittings and decorations.

A creative and flexible approach to this job is necessary, although other skills might come into play. For example, if you have an employee with bookkeeping experience you could contact accountants to take on extra bookkeeping as well as household chores. It is a good idea to make use of any business contacts if you have them - for example, if you know any event organisers, caterers or entertainers then you could suggest to companies that you organise their business conferences and office parties. Flexibility and common sense are a must, as you never know what jobs they might require.

The way a business like this one becomes really successful is through referrals. Once you get some work, get your client to refer you to their friends, neighbours, business colleagues and clients. Also, use previous clients as references - nothing generates extra trade better than good reports from others.

The rates you can charge are negotiable, but it is a good idea to set an hourly rate and charge accordingly. Bear in mind that your agency will be carrying out work for people who can afford to pay well for the services.

CHAPTER 34

Post-Construction Cleaning Agency

Offering a post-construction cleaning service is one way to take advantage of all the new houses, bungalows, flats and offices springing up all over the country. Once the building is completed, the builders are obliged to clear up the site, removing debris and possibly sweeping up, but their efforts tend to be cursory at best.

Imagine the dismay of any new owners having to make the effort to clear up before moving into their new house. The cleaning up may have been forgotten by the new owners in the frenzy of moving in, so having a ready cleaned house would reduce the stress of moving.

Think how much nicer it would be for them to move into a house with spotlessly clean walls and floors, ready for carpets to be laid. Paint work gleaming, windows sparkling, with toilet and bath shiny and clean. It could even be possible to tidy up the garden, with any weeds pulled up and lawns mown.

The way to find this kind of work for your agency is by approaching builders and builders' agents for contracts. There are plenty of these around, with many construction sites, so it should be possible to find firms who will book your agency and are willing to pay well for it.

Another source of work is estate agents. In a bid to become more competitive, estate agents have been offering home buyers better after sales service, including paying a visit after the sale with a small gift to thank people for their custom. One way estate agents could offer an even better service is by offering a pre-move house cleaning service, which is where you come in. This, of course, is not restricted to new houses, and can add another dimension to your service. Overall, a useful and lucrative service if marketed well.

CHAPTER 35

The "Do Anything" Manual Workers Agency

A business whose proposition is to do anything seems strange to say the least. Read on, however, and you will wonder why this kind of business isn't more common.

Consider the range of products that are manufactured today. The manufacture of over 95% of these products is handled, at least in part, by machines.

With the remaining 5% of these products, it is either too costly or too difficult to install machines to do the work. This means the production process has to be turned over to manual labour.

Given the ever changing nature of technology, demand and the market a company may require 100 people one day to work on a product, and then none the next. Hiring and firing on such a scale represents a big cost to the company, but given the lack of a cost effective alternative they have to do this.

Until now that is. A business employing a group of manual workers can profit from this situation. The do anything business can take on work from companies requiring anything from product assembly to envelope stuffing and deal with it in double quick time. This firm doesn't manufacture any of its own products and doesn't hold any stocks, but concentrates on handling manual work for other companies.

The key to this business is flexibility. The group of workers would handle pretty much any labour intensive task given to them, perhaps all working on the same thing, or doing something completely different.

Speed is another advantage offered by the do anything firm. If there were no deadlines, companies could afford to take on a few manual workers to do a task like product assembly. In the real world things don't work like that. When companies are given large orders that need to be completed overnight they can't rely on hiring their own labour - but they could rely on the do anything firm.

A flexible bank of anything from 20 to 200 workers could be kept occupied full time on labour intensive tasks. Things like soldering, packaging, assembling, addressing envelopes and correcting faults are always required by companies. If an order came in that needed dealing with immediately, tasks could easily be reorganised to cope. Occasionally, the level of orders might require taking on extra short term staff, although the firm could keep people on file for this eventually.

The do anything firm has certain similarities with temping agencies. However, it has advantages in that it deals primarily with labour intensive tasks where no skilled labour is needed, so suitable staff can always be found. In addition, it has its own premises, and is constantly on hand to deal with companies' requirements.

Production is increasingly being geared up to providing products just in time meaning that it is more common for companies to want large numbers of people quickly for short periods only, rather than employing a small number of people who are unoccupied half the time and then swamped when a big order comes in. There will always be a certain amount of jobs that machines can't do.

This business is undoubtedly a profitable one in any area close to light industry and commerce, and is going to be more and more in demand in the future.

CHAPTER 36

Temporary Clerical Work

Work Part Time And Run Your Own Business Too

The first two years of setting up a new business are usually the toughest. Extra income can make the difference between sailing effortlessly through the early days to grappling with constant cash flow problems.

A budding entrepreneur can guarantee a certain income while still providing enough time to develop the new business, by working as a part time clerical worker.

This opportunity is obviously open to anyone, but will be of particular interest to those about to swap the security of paid employment for the insecurity of working for themselves.

Read on and find out about one way to work part time and still find time to set up your own business.

Guaranteed Income

The idea of going out to find another job to support your own business might seem a little odd initially. There is no doubt that the best way to financially support a new self employment venture is by also finding some form of part time employment.

By doing this, you will have a guaranteed income. You can work at your new business with a safety net in place.

Trouble is, part time employment cannot always be easily fitted in around the things which must be done when trying to build a business. Clearly, few employers are going to allow people to pick and choose their hours.

There is also the problem of finding a part time job. There are plenty out there, but there are lots of people on the lookout for them as well. Don't worry - there is a form of part time work which is not too difficult to find and is extremely suitable for anyone trying to run a fledgling business - temporary clerical work.

A Godsend To New Entrepreneurs

Finding temporary clerical work through an agency could prove a godsend to new entrepreneurs. What we are talking about here is temporary clerical work with a difference.

Normally, temp. agencies tend to only be able to allocate temporary clerical work on a short term basis. Of course, it is different if you have a particular skill - such as keyboard or computer application experience - but if you don't then temporary clerical work can be a little irregular, and is often only handed out on a day to day basis.

While this might still be welcome for someone seeking income while their business is in an embryonic stage, it would be better if it were available on a more regular, or planned, basis.

There is a way to find temporary clerical work on a more regular basis if you keep your eyes open.

Regular Contracts

Nowadays large employment agencies often land contracts to tackle very big, but one off, clerical tasks. In order to fulfil these contracts, the agencies may recruit high numbers of staff through fairly low key advertising campaigns.

From these recruits, however, the agencies sometimes use the same people again and again. This is to their advantage because it means they don't have to spend so much time or money looking for fresh staff each time the need arises.

The advantage to you in being used in this way is that you can usually anticipate when you will be needed, and how long for. This need will frequently be for four or five weeks back to back.

Thus a new entrepreneur could plan periods when they can leave their business alone and go and earn some money elsewhere. Of course, if you needed to concentrate on your business for a while you could simply turn down any offers of temporary work.

So, anyone starting a business might be well advised to keep their eyes open for employment agencies advertising a need for temporary clerical staff.

It goes without saying that agencies will only employ people who can supply references and a National Insurance Number - and who appear reliable. They will also sometimes set applicants simple clerical tests to make sure they are up to the work. Other than that, the qualification criteria is not difficult to pass.

Temporary Work In Practice

A good example of the idea in practice occurred in London. Blue Arrow Personnel Services were engaged to handle all the returned voting papers in the Woolwich Building Society's conversion to a PLC. The work was fairly mundane - opening the envelopes and checking that the voting forms had been correctly filled in - but was carried out by a small army of temporary clerical staff, many of whom had been recruited for that purpose.

Among the army of staff were a few people who the agency had used a number of times before for similar projects. These people did not have to apply for each fresh contract Blue Arrow landed, but were automatically contacted by the agency with offers of work.

Some of these workers already had a pretty good idea of when they might be needed in the future. From experience they knew the kind of contracts Blue Arrow obtained and when the work would need to be carried out. To a degree they were able to plan their time knowing when they would be required for work and when they could concentrate on their business.

The normal occupations of these people ranged from acting to insurance loss adjustment. What they had in common was being self employed. The clerical work helped tide them over but allowed them to run their own businesses alongside.

Ideal

This work is ideal for individuals starting a business. Should that be you, either now or in the future, keep your eye open for employment agency advertisements looking for temporary clerical workers.

In those difficult early months of trading the opportunity to earn a regular income might be very welcome indeed. Apart from offering a financial lifeline, it might also put you in contact with people that turn out to be useful in the future. So don't delay - start looking for those advertisements right now!

And of course, instead of looking for part-time clerical work you could start-up your own employment agency.

CHAPTER 37

How Renting Can Make You Rich

How would you like to sell your product over and over again, but still own it?

This, in effect, is what hire companies do all the time. They purchase an item - often a quite expensive one - and then rent it out for a fee.

Not every product lends itself to hiring out and even fewer are suitable for the entrepreneur looking to set up at low cost. Here's why: people tend to rent things which they use infrequently, that are also expensive to buy.

We could all make money renting out luxury motorcars or industrial plants. They both satisfy the criteria, but how many of us could afford to obtain our stock in the first place!

Here's a rental business where the stock is dirt cheap and readily available, where your customers would far rather rent than buy.

Imagine you were having some friends come to stay for the weekend and these friends had a young child or baby. How well would you cope? Babies need an amazing array of paraphernalia and the parents would bring much of it with them. But what about a high chair, cot, play pen, fire guards, stair gate, pram, etc.? If you don't have young children, you are simply not geared up to have them in your home for much more than a flying visit.

Stock is readily available because, by the nature of the products, they are a transient requirement. Once the children outgrow them they become surplus to requirements and their value to the owners is diminished. What this means to you is that you can buy very cheaply.

Small advertisements in free newspapers and similar publications are a good place to obtain your stock. As you progress you may decide that some items would be better resold rather than rented out, which will provide another source of profit.

Once your business is established, you may decide to add other items to your stock. Toys and games are an obvious choice. Children's bikes are another.

With items such as these, your pay back time - the time it takes to get your money back in rental income - will be relatively short. Perhaps two or three rentals on some items. After that it's profit all the way.

In short, a great opportunity to make a second income from home.

CHAPTER 38

Classified Advertising Middle Man

Middle man opportunities are ideal for the lone entrepreneur looking for a way to make a part or full time income without investing capital, or taking any risks.

These opportunities arise where one party has a product or service to sell and another party is a potential customer for that product or service, but the two don't easily come into contact with each other. By forming a link between the seller and the potential buyer, the middle man can earn a sizeable commission without taking any risk or investing any of their own money.

They operate in practically every field of business. Sellers, with large amounts of capital invested, always welcome extra sales and anyone who can put them in touch with buyers they would never otherwise meet will be well rewarded. Some of the richest people in the world, achieved their wealth through acting as middle man, albeit on a grand scale.

This opportunity won't make you rich, but it is available for anyone to set up in any area of the UK without fuss or formality, and at minimal cost.

Newspapers carrying small advertisements placed by members of the public, exist in all areas. Pick up any local paper or free ads magazine and you will find both For Sale and Wanted ads for a vast range of products. Gather a number of these sources together and you'll discover that many of the items appearing in the For Sale ads can be matched up with items appearing as Wanted ads. This might not necessarily be in the same publication, but a match can easily be made.

Contact the person selling the item. Explain that you are an agent, and may have a buyer for the item. Agree a finder's fee (10 per cent of the price is reasonable) and then contact the potential buyer with details. You won't effect a sale every time, but all it will cost you is a couple of phone calls. On an expensive item, like a car, caravan or boat, the yield could be several hundred pounds. On a second hand three piece suite, it might only be £15 - £20, but still worth the phone calls.

This business works because people are naturally lazy. They'll place one local Wanted or For Sale ad and wait for the phone to ring. But by bringing together buyer and seller you can soon carve out a profitable niche for yourself.

CHAPTER 39

Sign Renewal Service

Take a look around your town or city, at its shops, factories, offices, pubs and other businesses. Are the signs well maintained? Or can you see a lot of signs where the paint is peeling off, or signs that are covered in graffiti?

If where you live or work looks more like the latter, don't get too upset at its shabby appearance. In fact, it represents a golden business opportunity to someone with a little artistic talent and some time to spare - working as a sign writer.

If you want to get into the sign writing business, a direct approach is probably best. If you see a business with some scruffy signs contact the boss and offer to repaint them on a weekend or evening, quoting them your price for the job. As long as the price is right, the convenience of you working when the business is closed means that they are very likely to accept the offer.

Get some business cards printed and distribute these to companies that are likely to require your services. Factories, offices and places like Council depots, for example, all require plenty of small basic signs where the kind of work will be fairly simple - for things like office doors, car parks, notice boards and directions. Thus, there is a lot of potential work available that will not be huge fancy signs, meaning that you do not have to necessarily have a great deal of experience in sign writing to set up in business.

You should find that the direct, personal approach will bring dividends. When you have done one job, personal recommendations can then bring extra business from other clients, or could lead to additional work with the same client. Keep in constant contact with potential clients, perhaps giving them a call every few months.

If you are new to the trade, are looking for additional marketing ideas, or are looking for additional information contact:

Signs (the official journal of the British Sign Association), Trent Press Ltd, Leen Gate, Lenton, Nottingham NG7 2LX.
or
Sign World, Stanley House, 9 West Street, Epsom, Surrey, KT18 7RL.

In terms of income, sign writing should bring in about £20 per hour. Your initial marketing will require a little time and effort but once you have done a few jobs your reputation will grow and additional business should come more easily. Although sign writing is an ideal job to begin on a part time basis working at evenings and weekends, it has the potential to escalate to a profitable full time occupation.

CHAPTER 40

Help Householders To Get Their Homes Looking Just How They Want Them

Shed Conversions

How many people do you know who have a dilapidated old hut at the bottom of their garden, which houses the lawnmower and an insect menagerie? Most people would rather holiday in Iraq than risk an Indiana Jones type encounter with giant spiders in their garden shed.

The potential for conversion, therefore, is huge. If you have the skills you could transform people's sheds into cosy guest houses, pet rooms or even a children's play area. Try your library for books containing ideas for shed conversions along with building and DIY tips.

Of course, it pays to know what you're doing. There are rigorous health and safety laws to negotiate and you won't get far by doing a second rate job. However, for those who can guarantee an inexpensive, professional service, the rewards could be massive.

Advertising in shop windows or the Yellow Pages will certainly attract customers, but better still, why not join an existing contractor? That way you can leave the paper work to them and get on with the important business of transforming that rusty old shed into a luxurious sauna.

Greenhouse Merchant

As more and more people turn their backs on Frankenstein foods, there's a growing demand for organic, home grown crops. After all, nobody wants to eat a carrot with eyes. By supplying prefabricated greenhouses you can offer people the chance to grow their own vegetables as nature intended and avoid the gene spliced mayhem of the supermarket shelves.

As a greenhouse retailer you will be able to supply and fit the frames (find a supplier who will supply them at trade prices). You can also advise people on which plants to grow and how to organise shelving for their greenhouse.

Besides being a practical alternative to a garden shed, a greenhouse can really enhance a garden. Colourful plants attract butterflies in the summer and create a perfect environment to relax in.

Create and Sell Outdoor Furniture

Outdoor furniture, although always popular, is rarely cheap. If you have a talent for carpentry and design, producing your own unique pieces of garden furniture can bring in a healthy profit.

Patio tables, benches, bird tables and ornaments can either be sold through adverts or to local garden centres. Hand crafted furniture is rare these days and commands premium prices, so you can expect a good return on all your hard work.

Your most likely supplier of materials will be a wholesale wood merchant. To save money and add interest, why not collect driftwood and logs from fallen trees and create garden furniture from them?

Yard Maintenance

Over time, many people's back yards become weed ridden rubbish tips. A rusted exercise bike stands as a lonely relic to that long forgotten fitness craze, while nomadic herds of crisp packets congregate around the twisted limbs of a decrepit barbecue.

You could make money transforming these desolate areas into an oasis of vegetation and beauty. If you enjoy working outside and have a basic knowledge of landscaping, yard maintenance and renovation could prove rewarding and financially viable. If you are a budding Alan Titchmarsh, with a good knowledge of garden flowers, shrubs and trees, even better.

The main things you will need are some regular garden tools and a creative eye. Consultations with the owners will give you a basic idea of what they'll be expecting and the rest is up to you. Once you have breathed life into your customer's back yard, make regular visits to maintain all that hard work and effort.

As with all of these ventures, it is a good idea to get business cards printed to give to customers to pass to friends.

CHAPTER
41

Local Guides

Here's an ideal opportunity for holidays and weekends. Whenever we visit a town where we haven't been before, one of the first things we do, whether we're there on holiday or simply to do a bit of shopping, is find out where to go and what to do.

We want to know where all the places of interest are, such as the best places to shop and how to get there, or whether there are any interesting walks to go on, or interesting things we can see and do.

Most towns, whether they are well known tourist centres or not, will have tourist information centres people can visit. If you're new to a place, finding the tourist information office may be problematic - we might not have a map, we might not be able to find a parking space, or the place might simply be too busy and crowded for us to be bothered. Even if we do find it, we are usually faced with piles of leaflets which we have to sort through and make sense of.

This business is one which will solve all these problems. It can be operated in any town or city, or even in the countryside so long as there are a few people about, and requires very little in the way of start up costs and running expenses.

It requires gathering together information on your local town or area and packaging it together in a handy guide. All you need is a little knowledge of your locality. Such a guide should include things like where to go, parks, beaches, shops, museums, cinemas and theatres, sports centres and fairs; where to eat and stay; information on buses and parking, and anything else that might be useful, either to the visitor or the local.

The best way to sell your guide is on foot, selling to tourists coming out of train and bus stations, or to people in shopping centres or outside other tourist attractions. You could get shops to stock your guides, but selling directly to tourists on foot cuts out the problem of them having to find the tourist information office, and you should find that a certain proportion of locals will buy them too. You could also sell them through hotels and B&Bs.

If you live in the country, or in a place not particularly renowned for tourism, then a good idea is to put together a list of interesting walks. These could be of varying length, perhaps grouped according to ease and accessibility, describing the route and what people will see along the way. It's amazing how many people enjoy a good walk, and this has an advantage in that local people as well as tourists will buy guides of this type.

You won't necessarily need any writing skills. Even a straight duplicate of a local bus timetable can be sold to passers by who can't be bothered to visit the bus station, or who don't want to pay for a more expensive guide in a shop. Ideally though, you should write a few words describing any place of interest, which can be based on the wording from their own leaflets and promotional guides. Try to include a map - a simple hand drawn one will do.

It won't cost you a lot of money in production costs either. It is best to write your guide using a word processor, from which a cheap A4 or A5 black and white booklet can easily be printed or photocopied. With potential production costs of 15p per 20 page A5 guide, and an easy to sell at retail price of £1, that's a profit of 85p per guide.

If your guide is of reasonable quality, and you go out most weekends, you should be easily able to sell 10,000 copies a year in a reasonable tourist area just by yourself. When you take into account the other sales opportunities, and the 85p profit per guide, then £8,500 plus income per year should be well within reach.

CHAPTER 42

Customised Calendars
Make And Earn Yourself A Happy New Year!

Here's a novel low cost business opportunity that could really give you a Merry Christmas and a Happy New Year: customised calendars.

What you do is to invite people to send in 12 of their favourite photos, which you then turn into a customised calendar. People will pay premium prices for a personalised gift such as this, and you won't need much capital to set up and run this business either.

Firstly, you need to put together a standard format 12 page A4 sized calendar, with a space on each page for a 6" x 4" photograph. Printers and copy shops will do this for you if you explain what you require. Alternatively, if you or a friend has a computer with desktop publishing or word processing software then you can produce a template calendar very easily and inexpensively.

Once you have your template, producing each customer's personalised calendar is easy. Once they send in their photos you simply reproduce each page using a colour photocopier, placing each separate photograph in the space provided.

This makes for a colourful, quality looking but inexpensive calendar, that will give you a healthy profit mark up!

To market your service, advertise in suitable newspapers and magazines, and/or gift shops. Your advertising should invite people to send in their photos (explain that you will return them) along with their payment and personal details so you can mail the calendar back to them.

You can charge £15 to £20 for each calendar, which should be printed on good quality gloss paper. Your production, marketing and distribution costs should be less than half the final retail price, which will give you an idea of how profitable this venture can be.

There are various ways to expand the business so that you can earn money throughout the year. Customised birthday, anniversary and Christmas cards could be made using your customers' favourite personal photographs, and you could also produce personalised novelty posters, photograph albums and even wrapping paper using the same basic idea.

This simple and low cost business could be exactly the earner you need. If you get started today, the money you make could really lift your Christmas spirits and set you up for the New Year.

CHAPTER 43

Floor Advertisements
Eyes Down For A New Advertising
Opportunity

Advertising, to be successful, relies on being eye catching and highly visible. Hence advertisers fight to get the best spots for their ads on walls and advertising hoarding in busy spots that will be seen by thousands every day.

Competition is so fierce that advertisers are constantly looking for better and more original sites for their ads - such as on ceiling panels, an exciting idea with huge potential.

Now another advertising innovation has sprung up - floor ads. These are laminated posters stuck to the floors of supermarkets and other stores, that are seen by customers as they make their way around the store. In terms of popularity, floor ads are rapidly gaining ground on the more standard forms of instore advertising like wall panels.

Durable and eye catching floor ads are good for the shops because they can profitably utilise dead floor space, earning a small amount of cash for each ad carried. More importantly, selling floor advertising space represents a superb business, that if handled properly can be set up cheaply and easily run by one or more people.

The great thing about this business is the relatively high prices you can charge clients for advertising. Although you will have to pay shops for the privilege of displaying the ads, as well as paying for the materials to make the ad, these costs will be more than swallowed up by the amount you can charge advertisers to display their ads, meaning that big profits can be earned.

How does it work? There are three distinct stages: locating advertising sites, finding advertisers and then making and installing the signs.

To begin with you will have to find suitable shops to advertise in. Supermarkets and certain large stores are ideal, as they have plenty of floor space and plenty of customers who will wander around and see the ads. These shops will also tend to be better disposed than others towards having large display ads on their floor.

Depending upon their in-store decor not all shops will want floor ads, but the fact that they will be earning money from previously non utilised space - without any effort on their part - should guarantee that many stores will take you up on your offer. So shop around, concentrating on large stores (particularly the kind of warehouse and factory shops you find in retail parks), supermarkets, and any other sites you can think of, showing them examples of your ads, and you should generate some interest. Don't forget to agree on a display fee, based upon the amount of space used.

Once you have one or more suitable sites you need to find clients who wish to advertise. This could be anybody, advertising just about any product or service, so spread your marketing net widely. Think about where the ad is situated. In a large chain of DIY stores for example, you could advertise a DIY product.

Alternatively, in a local supermarket you could advertise other local shops, services, places to go, and so on. By matching the ad with the site, and reminding the advertiser of the numbers of people who will see it, you should get plenty of customers.

Finally, you will need to make the floor ad. First you need to obtain the client's artwork for the ad. Laminated self adhesive vinyl, which can be obtained from the company 3M should be used as a covering for the advertisement, being clear and durable. The vinyl should be slightly larger than the ad itself, so that it can be stuck to the floor. Be sure to obtain quality materials - poor presentation will mean fewer clients, although large and well known companies will pay highly for a quality ad.

You should charge clients according to the duration and size of the ad. Let's say you charge £100 per sq. ft. per month (although depending on the site/client you could charge a great deal more). For a six foot square poster sized ad you would earn £600 to display it for a month. In addition, let's say you pay the shop £180 a month to display it (£30 per ft. per month), and the materials cost £20 - total costs of £200. This gives you a healthy profit of £400.

Of course, the amounts you can charge clients and the amounts you will have to pay shops to display the ads will vary according to their prestige. For example, you would probably pay more to display an ad in a large chain DIY store than in a local supermarket, but you could charge more for it, resulting in bigger profits. The above is only a basic example, but it illustrates the potential of this venture, particularly when you consider the large numbers of possible sites and advertisers.

Although shop floor ads are a new idea, they are starting to catch on. A UK firm called Eyes Down has had some success with the idea, getting appointed as sole representative for floor advertising in 55 outlets of the wholesale chain Nurdin and Peacock, and has also been successful selling the idea abroad.

Now is the time to get involved in this business, as there is little competition. Few retailers currently know about the benefits of floor ads, and you could be the person to sell the idea to them. You might find that while their customers are looking down, your business prospects are rocketing skyward.

CHAPTER 44

Selling Second Hand
Books And Magazines

Many people make the mistake of thinking that any money making opportunity worth considering must be new. It simply isn't the case.

Some opportunities just keep rolling on year after year after year, and the reason is this: they offer a benefit to the customer which satisfies an ongoing need. Here's an interesting example.

Buy stock for virtually nothing!
Sell it to collectors for huge profits!

Millions of pounds worth of books and magazines are purchased every year. Once they've been read they tend to be either thrown away or confined to some dusty corner of the attic. The value to the original purchaser is practically zero. They've read the publication already. That doesn't mean that no one else would be interested. There is, and always will be, a market for second hand books and magazines. They're cheap and easy to buy, and they're ideal for profit.

On one side you have a group of people whose only choice is to either throw their books and magazines away, or sell them to you. What do you suppose that does to the purchase price? On the other hand, you have a potential market who value the product highly, they haven't read it yet, and might be desperately seeking what you're selling. This makes for an excellent profit potential.

Most efforts at selling secondhand books and magazines are confined to disposing of unwanted items at car boot sales. This is obviously a good source of low priced stock. Just remember that no one wants to take anything home from a car boot sale, and make offers accordingly. Rock bottom is the order of the day.

What separates the amateur, who makes a few pounds from his junk on a Sunday, from the professional who makes a tidy ongoing income, is marketing and presentation.

No one likes to buy dog eared books or magazines. Make sure your stock is well presented, put it in a cellophane or plastic protective sleeve, and you'll multiply the value. Most products appear more valuable if they're packaged properly. Second-hand magazines and books are no exception.

In terms of marketing, car boot sales, market stalls and flea markets are just three possibilities. This is also an ideal mail order opportunity.

It's even possible to work this business locally from a room in your house. Place cheap advertisements in your local newsagents along the lines of "Second-hand books and Magazines bought and sold". Buy at price X and sell for 3X. The great thing about working in this way is that your buyers will also become your suppliers and vice versa. You simply act as intermediary, taking a slice of profit for your trouble.

You could deal in all magazines and books, or you might decide to specialise in a particular field. Specialisation is ideal for a mail order operation. By placing advertisements in the relevant magazines you can easily attract buyers and sellers.

This is an excellent business to tie in with an interest or hobby. Dealing in secondhand publications related to a hobby or field of interest is a very good way of mixing business with pleasure.

As with any business of this type, the hardest part will be getting started, making people aware that you exist. Once this has been achieved, repeat business should be plentiful. Even though the product sells for a relatively small amount, a single customer could be worth £100 or more profit each year. Consider this example.

Let's say you specialise in cookery magazines. Your customer comes to you with 10 magazines they've already read and wants to buy 10 others you have in stock. You buy the old magazines for 30p each and sell the new ones for £1 each. You've made £7 profit straight away, and have 10 new magazines to sell (with a potential profit of another £7).

Next month your customer comes back. He wants to sell back the magazines he bought last month, and buy 10 new ones. Another £7 profit for you, and you've got the original magazines back to resell. Build a business with 100 customers like this and you'll be making tremendous profits. Even something a little more modest will yield a nice part time income.

Everyone wins with this kind of deal. You're making a profit, and your customer gets to read lots of books/magazines at a fraction of the new cost. The secondhand book and magazine business is simplicity itself to run. The rules are clear. Buy stock cheaply from someone who has no further use for it, and sell it at a nice profit to someone who wants it.

Here's an opportunity which will never go away. Don't overlook it just because it's been around for ever, and it's so simple. The best things in life usually are.

CHAPTER 45

How To Stay In The World's Top Hotels For Free And Make A Healthy Living!

Travelling the world, visiting cosmopolitan capitals, exotic resorts and being pampered in the best hotels is something most people can only dream of. To say you could be doing this for free and even make a profit from it without having won the Lottery or the Pools sounds unbelievable, but it is true.

A Pleasurable and Profitable Business

The way to do this is to set up this lucrative offshoot of the tourist industry. It is an idea that requires effort and straightforward common sense, but works and can be extremely pleasurable and profitable in the right hands. Travelling, enjoyable as it is, is only a by-product of the business, and in fact you don't necessarily need to go anywhere to make money from it.

The idea is to write, publish and market a guide to the world's best hotels, detailing their facilities and standards, adding information about hotel service, haute cuisine, its location, and convenience regarding airports and railway stations. It will take a little effort to establish, but once this is done the rewards are enormous.

See The World For Free, And Make Money

The business has some obvious perks. Once you have made contact with the hotel explaining the nature of the publication and potential demand in precise detail, you can look forward to top service, accommodation and the best cuisine.

There are additional rewards. A guide to the world's best hotels is beneficial to both the hotel and the traveller. The revenue from such a publication can be huge. This is achieved by the sales of the guide through normal book selling outlets. Additional revenue comes from international advertisers. You can create a publishing structure which builds in a guaranteed income selling to individual hotels or the larger chains.

Establishing The Guide

Your first step is to contact the hotels in order to let them know the benefits of participating, and establishing the reputation of your business. Prepare a detailed questionnaire that is fair and relevant. It is important this questionnaire is targeted at the big chains and bookers who will encourage their clients to participate and agree to an entry in the guide. Once an entry is agreed, you can discuss the time and duration of a visit.

Guaranteed Income

The next step is where the guaranteed element of sales revenue is secured. The establishments are asked to accept an agreed number of copies at a discounted rate, which they would give as complimentary copies to favoured clients. Thus, if the cover price is, for example £16, the guide could be offered to participants for £11.

You may find a few establishments may not wish to accept this part of the deal, but most will and in doing so will generate a substantial cash flow. For instance, if each hotel accepted 15 guides at £11 each and you had visited 400 hotels, that would create an income potential of 400 x 15 guides x £11 per copy, totalling £66,000.

Remember that £66,000 is without any retail revenue or advertising income. It is a guaranteed income because participating hotels will have signed an acceptance form which commits them to taking an agreed number of guides prior to publication.

Other Sales Options

You can add in more dimensions to potential sales and revenue. High Street book shops may certainly be interested and there is an excellent opportunity for setting up your own mail order sales operation.

If you find the prospect of travelling tiresome, remember not every hotel entry has to be personally vetted. All potential clients will publish either press packs or more modest brochures and all the essential information to fit your guide format can be gleaned from these. It may be appropriate to do some on the spot observations, but you could always send another representative of your business.

Once you have confirmation of firm orders from the hotels you are then in an excellent position to project costs and profits of a publication always on the move, in need of frequent updating, and, by definition, well capable of picking up repeat sales as well as new readers.

And, of course, potential sales from all sources can be maximised by creating an international distribution system. The whole idea can be adjusted and fine tuned to your own circumstances and requirements.

Putting The Guide Together

When you have gathered together as much information as necessary, through your questionnaires, on the spot observations and the hotels' press and publicity material, it will be time to put together the guide.

Obviously you need to be able to write in a clear, informative and objective manner, but you don't need to be an aspiring Pullitzer Prize winner to do this.

Be generous with the text and pictures of each hotel - one colour page per hotel is a reasonable allocation of space. Design, typesetting and printing are no problem, because many good quality printers now have an in house design team, who will work to your brief and supply written quotations.

Sit Back and Enjoy the Profits

By this time, all the spade work will have been done, and actually writing the guide will seem like the easy part. All the information will have been gathered, your sales and distribution network established and the benefits of appearing in your guide clearly explained to all the participating hotels.

It is this aspect which requires time and effort, but always remember the perks this business can bring. There can be few more alluring businesses than one where the travelling, wining and dancing tab is picked up, not by you, but your clients, you get to see the world for free, and still make a profit!!

CHAPTER 46

CV Writing Using a Computer

In these days where a job vacancy might attract hundreds, perhaps thousands, of applications, the need for a professionally written and produced CV (curriculum vitae) has never been greater. Many applicants either do not know how to put together a CV or do not have the right equipment to do so. A CV writing service is therefore something that will be in great demand, and it is an easy and inexpensive service to set up.

All you will need is word processing software and a printer, plus knowledge of how to put together an effective CV. You need to obtain from each customer this standard information, which will form the various sections of the CV: personal details (name, address, telephone number, marital status, nationality, driving licence), qualifications (education, training, courses), career history and spare time interests.

The best CVs are concise and tailored towards the jobs the individual is applying for. This can mean producing various different CVs for one person, which helps to boost your revenue.

To promote your service, advertise in local and national newspapers and trade magazines. Do not forget this is a service you can operate by post, so spread your marketing net widely. It is well worth having cards printed to leave on notice boards at places like job centres, careers centres, enterprise agencies, employment agencies, personnel departments, colleges and libraries. It is also a good idea to produce leaflets to send to people who enquire about the service, perhaps incorporating a questionnaire so that clients can fill in their personal details - don't forget to ask what kind of jobs they are applying for.

When you produce a CV, charge between £10 and £14, which will more than cover the cost of producing one master CV and five copies. You can charge extra for further copies. Profitable add ons to this service are writing covering letters, and supplying quality paper and envelopes to enhance the applicant's presentation.

CHAPTER
47

Absentee Home Seller Service

Selling a house can be easier if you're still living there. You can turn up the heating, put out fresh flowers and have some fresh coffee on the brew to seduce buyers.

Trouble is, many owners have to move out of the area before they can sell, while others can't spare the time to show people around, so the property ends up fetching far less than the asking price. An empty house is unappealing to a prospective buyer, and a dark, cold one is even worse - the amenities will have been disconnected if the owner has moved out.

The absentee home seller's service is the answer here - someone to do all the jobs the owner isn't around to do, but which don't fall under the remit of the estate agent.

So each time someone comes to view the property you are on hand to turn on the heating, open the windows, show people around while emphasising the property's good points (which representatives of the estate agent don't tend to do, surprisingly) and make the place look attractive and appealing. You could also clear out left behind furniture, oddments and rubbish, and even add a lick of paint here and there.

Without this service the owner may be forced to accept a price 10% lower than expected (e.g. £54,000 for a house worth £60,000). With it, however, they can easily achieve well above the asking price.

Your fee of 3% of the house price, plus expenses, is therefore more than reasonable (you'd charge £1,800 for overseeing the sale of a £60,000 property, for example).

Advertising in the property section of local newspapers is the obvious way to get custom from house vendors. You could also try calling on properties recently placed on the market, or dropping your business card/leaflet through the letterbox.

Another possibility is to work in partnership with estate agents. Get them to recommend your service to their customers in return for a commission on your fee.

As well as costing virtually nothing to start, this service fulfils a need that isn't currently catered for.

CHAPTER
48

Rentable Property Agent

Finding somewhere to live can be a hassle, especially to someone moving from outside the area.

In any town or city there are always plenty of properties available, but the problem is finding the right one. There will be umpteen estate agents to contact, property small ads to check, and shop windows with "To Rent" cards in to look at.

Following up these sources is time consuming, inconvenient and expensive, meaning there is a real need for a service providing a "one stop shop" for people seeking rented accommodation.

This is another easy, low cost start up. Your job will be to gather together all the available information on properties to rent in your town/area on a weekly basis. So put yourself on estate agents' mailing lists, read the local property press, keep an eye on the ads in shop windows, and keep this up to date information in a file.

When clients contact you, ask for their details - where they want to live, number of people, the amount they're prepared to pay - and compile a list of suitable properties (a word processor or computer database will be useful here). The list could, of course, be posted to the client.

Charge a finder's fee of 50p per property on the list (£5 minimum charge). Clients will pay readily because you're saving them the bother of finding all the estate agents' numbers, ringing around, and looking in lots of shop windows and newspapers, plus the time and expense of making lots of property finding trips.

This service has obvious potential in any town or city, especially student towns. Advertise in the main newspapers as well as the business and student press, and put up posters and signs to promote your enterprise.

CHAPTER 49

Vegetable Landscapes
Are A Fertile Enterprise

Boston based Susan Power Dalton left her job as a lawyer to turn her hobby into a full time business, showing that landscaping gardens can be fertile ground for aspiring entrepreneurs

You've probably noticed that the fad for house makeover programmes on television has spread to the garden.

If you've ever seen shows such as Ground Force, Garden Doctors, Home Front in the Garden and Gardening Neighbours, you'll have enjoyed watching people's gardens being transformed from weed strewn bombsites into lushly landscaped paradises to rival Kew Gardens.

Envy Of The Neighbourhood

Anyone who can offer this service will be in real demand. While practically everyone would love to have an attractive garden, it is a job few can do on their own. The transformation would require designing and landscaping, choosing the right plants, planting them, and a great deal of additional work.

Not many people can put in the time and effort required, and even less actually have the necessary expertise. But a substantial number would be happy to pay a professional to turn their garden into the envy of the neighbourhood.

Lifelong Hobby

Susan Power Dalton of Boston offers such a service. For a fee she will redesign her client's garden, install beds and features, and plant vegetables, plants and flowers.

She can also be hired to return for subsequent plantings and consultation, and even for a garden cleanup.

A qualified lawyer, Dalton set up her company, Vegetable Landscapes, a year and a half ago. Dissatisfied with law practice, she decided to pursue her lifelong hobby, and it has paid off. Her average commission runs into hundreds of dollars and she enjoys her work immensely.

To publicise the business 12,000 flyers were sent out. This approach appears to have worked - Vegetable landscapes is becoming popular with Boston's professionals, many of whom have never had a vegetable garden before. Forty gardens were planted last year, but this year Dalton aims to plant one hundred and twenty. Sometimes clients ask her to create a garden as a gift or house-warming present for someone else.

Designing The Garden

Dalton designs her gardens on the computer. She has developed three standard packages:

☒ A 4 x 4 with bamboo tower and 12 herbs and salad vegetables. This package costs $395 (around £250).

☒ A 4 x 12 with bamboo towers and 30 vegetables, herbs and flowers at $995 (about £620).

☒ A 12 x 12 with two bamboo towers, a trellis and 50 herbs, flowers and vegetables for $1,995 (approximately £1,250).

They sound expensive, but the advantage of having standardised packages is that it simplifies marketing and makes sourcing materials and plants more cost effective, so as a result the prices are extremely competitive. However, Dalton will modify the designs and even develop completely customised gardens if required.

Rewarding and Therapeutic

Susan Power Dalton's experience in running her own business proves that anyone with enough gardening know how could easily set up a similar operation. So start planning yours now, in time for next Spring. As well as being incredibly rewarding and therapeutic, garden landscaping and installation can be a hugely profitable full time operation or second income opportunity.

CHAPTER 50

Personalised, Customised And Tailor Made Goods And Services

People love goods that make them feel unique, special and important. Goods customised for a particular person are much more likely to be purchased than their generic versions.

When buying a present for someone it is far better to give something personalised to the recipient. How much better to receive a tailor made gift, implying that the present has been painstakingly researched and sought out, and making the occasion that much more special.

Personalised goods represent a big untapped market. Only a certain number of tastes and personalities can be catered for by mass manufactured and marketed goods. By offering a service on demand to certain people, you can offer a unique product, and charge for it accordingly.

There is an unlimited number of goods that could be personalised, customised and tailor made, and an unlimited number of ways you could do it. If you have a particular skill, hobby or interest, you could make some money out of it by selling goods and services on demand to particular people.

Alternatively, many of these ideas involve customising goods already manufactured - generally a very easy task. Here are 20 of the best and most profitable ideas for businesses concerned with personalised goods you could run.

Every Day Household Objects

It is possible to personalise all kinds of household objects, if you have the right equipment. It is possible to print onto certain items, but a better idea is to use print transfers to emboss text onto goods. For example, you can add initials, names, addresses or other text onto goods such as pens, briefcases, suitcases, diaries, notebooks, golf and snooker cues, or practically anything else. If you are able to sew, you can do the same for clothes, towels, handkerchiefs or any material.

You could also offer a service to businesses, clubs, or any organisation, embroidering logos, initials, names and insignia onto items such as ties, napkins and handkerchiefs. Produce a catalogue of products and advertise your services in up-market publications, perhaps offering a free gift as an incentive.

Pet Products

People tend to dote on their pets and you can take advantage of this by selling personalised pet products. For example, pet names could be added to identity tags, collars, feeding bowls, baskets and blankets. Again, produce a catalogue of products and advertise in shop windows, local newspapers and specialised pet magazines.

Christmas Cards

An excellent idea is to sell packs of Christmas cards with text printed on the front saying, for example, "The Jones family wish you a very Happy Christmas". You can modify ready manufactured cards or create your own, combining the text with a picture. Contact customers by picking surnames from the telephone directory and selling by direct mail.

Pictures of Houses

If you have the ability to paint well, a lucrative idea is to paint pictures of people's houses. It may take time and you may require various sittings, but you can charge well for this service. It is best to concentrate your efforts on more affluent areas, and it is best to offer a framing service too.

Portraits and Caricatures

Another idea requiring artistic ability is to draw personal portraits, sketches or humorous caricatures, depending on your style and talent. You could call on households showing examples of your work, although you will be more likely to generate business by setting up a stall in a busy shopping centre, thoroughfare or tourist attraction. If you can't draw, team up with an artist. You do the marketing, they do the artwork.

Poems

Composing poems to order will make a memorable and unique gift for any special occasion, such as birthdays, weddings, engagements, anniversaries, births, and so on. It is possible to write just one poem and insert different names, or other personal details. This is particularly easy if you have a computer and printer, although if you have calligraphy skill you can have the poem hand written, mounted and framed. Advertise your service in newspapers and magazines and send the poems out by direct mail. Alternatively, set up a stall in a shopping centre, fair or tourist attraction and compose poems on the spot. There is a guy who sells poems for £1 under Waterloo Bridge in London. I estimate he takes £300- £500 a day in cash!

T-Shirts

Personalised T-shirts are likely to be popular items, particularly in the summer months. It is possible to purchase fabric paints and sprays very cheaply, or you can offer a screen printing service. By creating stencils of letters you can print out text very easily, or if you have the artistic ability, you could create pictures and logos too. This is a business you can run from home by mail order and advertise accordingly. You could also set up a stall in a market or fair and offer a "while you wait" service.

Forms and Certificates

Businesses, clubs and other organisations are always in need of forms, whether standard invoices, petty cash receipts or time sheets, or more personalised forms and certificates. A service offering both standard business forms, including things like the company address, or more personal paperwork, is ideal if you have artistic ability and/or computer graphics and word processing software. You can even expand your service to include producing company logos, menus and advertisements. Produce a catalogue and advertise your service in various publications.

Signs

People often require signs, whether for house names, personal names for affixing to bedroom doors, or various business related signs such as office name plates, factory areas, shop names and Vacancy/No Vacancy signs. You can offer a 'while you wait' sign making service for personal customers at craft fairs, markets and tourist attractions. You could also lease part of a shop to make your signs, creating a catalogue in order to market your signs to businesses.

Ghost Writing

If you have writing and editing ability, you can run a ghost writing business, rewriting CV and job applications, or rewriting stories and articles the original writer wishes to sell under their own name. An extension of this could be to write or ghost write biographies, which could make an imaginative birthday, retirement or anniversary gift.

Advertising Space

By leasing a prominent wall space in a town or city, you can charge people for the creation and display of their own personal message. People may wish to give birthday or anniversary congratulations, or even messages of love or marriage proposal. You could use large display letters that are easily changed, or paint the messages on. Keep the messages clean, and charge a daily or weekly fee.

Jewellery

Jewellery is a popular item, particularly for women, and whether bought by people for themselves or as a present for somebody else, there is a big market for personalised jewellery. There are no limits to what you could create if you have the skill and materials, but many items can be made easily and cheaply using wood, wire, and gold and silver plated jewellery attachments. Wooden jewellery is ideal, as it has become very popular, and can be carved very easily. You can create brooches with first names on, or earrings, bangles, bracelets and pendants, of any design. Set up a market stall and sell by mail order, advertising your products in women's magazines, the local press and shop windows.

Outfits

Putting together and designing outfits is a service likely to be popular with businesses and individuals alike. You can put together weird and wonderful costumes for special promotions, even providing the people to wear them if necessary. Businesses often have corporate makeovers, so you can make money by designing outfits to suit. Alternatively, you could design and make fashionable clothes, tailor made to individual tastes. You should advertise your service to advertising and public relations agencies and local theatre companies, as well as advertising in suitable publications and putting up stylish posters in shopping centres, cafes and venues.

Confectionery

Novelty and personalised confectionery will make an unusual and exciting gift for both adults and children. You do not necessarily need a thorough knowledge of confectionery manufacturing - there are a number of chocolate and icing based products where all you will require is to be able to add icing to a product. Another idea is to create your own moulds to make interesting and varied shapes. You could even sell rock with a name, or "I am X years old", running through the centre.

Jingles, Music and Sound-Bites

Disc Jockeys like to create their own personal sound and style, and one way they do this is through the use of their own memorable jingles. If you have the necessary equipment you can easily create jingles to order, perhaps recording them yourself, or taking and recording sound bites from films, radio or the television (taking into account copyright restrictions). Creating audio cassettes and CDs containing jingles for all occasions and selling them to shops or by mail order is a good way of selling your products. You can also produce specific jingles for particular customers. A related area is to produce musical backing tracks for films, business and educational videos, slide shows and exhibitions. Again, you can produce cassettes or CDs of music for all occasions, or produce music specific to one client. Advertise your service in audio-visual equipment and arts related magazines.

Novelty Posters and Certificates

These are fun products with a lot of sales potential. Novelty posters and certificates make excellent gifts for birthdays, anniversaries and special occasions, such as a work colleague leaving or getting a promotion. If you have computer word processing and/or desktop publishing software, plus a printer these products will be very easy to manufacture. Use your imagination and you will be able to think of all kinds of products, but you could start with joke passports. Advertise and sell them in joke, novelty and gift shops.

Songs

Writing and recording personalised songs can be a money spinner if you have the talent and equipment. You can produce songs for all occasions, such as birthdays, engagements, weddings, births and anniversaries, which should include a name (or two) repeated within the song. It is possible to write and record one song for a birthday, re-recording the vocal part for different names. You can also record one off songs for specific clients. Sell by mail order, using classified ads in local newspapers and the music press to attract orders, or produce cassettes and CDs for particular names to be sold in gift and toy shops.

Cocktails

Specially devised cocktails and punches will make a unique gift and help pep up any party. The service should offer a special personalised recipe card plus a certain amount of ready made cocktails, or a big bowl of punch. You can create and sell these to both individuals and businesses, naming the drink after the person nominated by the purchaser or sponsor. Advertise in the local press and party shops to build up your orders.

Crests

In the past, every respectable family had their own crest, and today there is a market for selling family, business or college crests, painted onto wooden plaques. Research should enable you to discover a source of reference for old family crests, and if this shows that certain family names do not have one, you can even design them. There is also scope for selling to businesses, organizations and colleges. Sell by mail order, finding potential customers by locating surnames and businesses in the Yellow Pages or similar.

Stickers

Personalised self adhesive stickers for children to add to toys and books, address labels, or identity labels to attach to suitcases, or even household goods, are all popular and necessary items. You could design and produce a range of stickers containing children's first names, or similar other items. These can then be sold in toy shops, gift and novelty shops, or by mail order.

Other Ideas

- ☒ tapestries of logos, family names and family histories
- ☒ time capsules
- ☒ tourist site pictures
- ☒ life history photos
- ☒ relationship assessments
- ☒ business and personal mottos

CHAPTER
51

House Clearance
With A Difference

An extra dimension to a simple house clearance service could earn you £1,000 plus in revenue per house. Rather than merely stripping houses and moving belongings on behalf of private customers, you could work on behalf of solicitors providing a total probate evaluation and house clearance service.

Probate evaluation involves checking a person's Will when they die and establishing who gets what. It doesn't require in depth legal knowledge - any retailer or antiques enthusiast can easily learn it.

Solicitors are swamped by this kind of work, but tend to prefer dealing with more prestigious contracts, preferring to sub contract probate and house clearance jobs. Your service can kill two birds with one stone by establishing probate when someone dies, before clearing the house and ensuring that the items within go to their rightful places.

For clearing a big house you can earn in excess of £1,000. For an average sized house you will probably earn between £500 and £600.

There is a lot of probate work about. When people die, someone has to deal with the Will and sort out the house and its contents, and relatives often live many miles away. You would take on the Will of the recently deceased on behalf of the solicitor, make an inventory of the premises and value it for probate purposes. Your next task is to remove any bequeathed items and ensure that they get to the correct friend or relation. Then you take any valuables to an antiques auction room, take less valuable items to a salesroom and dump anything else. Finally, you would arrange to have the house cleaned before it is put up for sale or reoccupied.

Contact solicitors to see if they have any clearance and probate work available. Be persistent and offer good references and it will really pay off.

CHAPTER
52

Specialty Second Hand Shopping

Second hand goods shops, exchange shops and charity goods shops are all businesses that we have seen, if not used. Currently they are very popular, highlighting the level of demand for secondhand goods, although these outlets have been around for years.

These shops all sell just about every type of second hand product you can think of under one roof, from clothes to compact disk players, bric a brac to business computers, ranging from the good quality to the downright shoddy.

An idea now popular across the USA is that of setting up specialist second hand shops. These shops sell only one type of second hand product, making them a one stop shop for specialist items such as computers, musical equipment, stereo and audio equipment, sports goods and toys and children's goods.

The advantages of this type of shop are twofold. Firstly, how many people would give away unwanted items to charity shops when they knew they would be able to get something for them at their local second hand shop?

Secondly, by adding in competitively priced brand new merchandise you would then be offering your customers the best of both worlds, rather like car dealers offer a choice in either used or new cars. This gives the shop an extra attraction, removes the down market element of secondhand shopping and attracts customers from a much bigger range for each one stop shop.

You will need a reasonable idea of what to select for sale and what not to, and how much to pay for your secondhand goods. You can read trade magazines, classified ad magazines such as Exchange & Mart, and check wholesale and retail prices to examine the market for different goods and gauge what prices to pay and what to charge.

The key to the success of this idea is to carefully select your second hand items so that they look good and, in the case of electrical products, perform well. Once again, you will need to have a reasonable idea of what an item does, how it works, and if it works, particularly with electrical goods, but you certainly do not need to be an expert to do this.

Your customers will also need to be able to examine the goods, checking that they work and that they do what they want them to do. It may not be possible to demonstrate every product sold in the shop, so a way of overcoming this problem is to offer a full refund if product is returned with 48 hours deal. This gives the customer enough time to check that their purchase is working and, very importantly, provides peace of mind when buying. Ultimately, this means that the con merchant image of some second hand vendors is dispelled from customers' minds and you sell more products.

Here are a few examples of the type of business you could run.

Sporting Equipment

Sporting equipment is a massive growth sector these days, where mums and dads are just as likely to buy tennis rackets, golf clubs and ice skates as their fitness conscious offspring. People take up sports and drop them again regularly, so there is likely to be a huge supply of second hand equipment. The core of the business would be based on stocking a varied selection of good quality used equipment, enhanced by an equally diverse range of new sports gear and accessories.

Computers

How many households do not have a computer these days? How many different levels of sophisticated technology are there? It follows that there are always plenty of people just starting on the ladder of computer use and just as many, if not more, who are constantly looking to upgrade their systems. Again, the correct mix of used and new products should be very attractive to potential purchasers. In the same field but with the potential to develop as a business in itself is providing a specialist outlet for computer software of all types, for all computer systems.

CDs, Records and Videos

These are all popular, with great potential for second hand sales.

Children's Goods

Can you think of a shop near you which provides high class used and new children's goods? If you can't, you are staring at a big hole in the market, which you can fill by selling toys, clothes, books and furniture to those concerned with the needs of children. Kids often grow out of clothes and toys before they wear out, so there is likely to be a good supply. It is a simple idea, but one with excellent prospects.

Musical Instruments

The music industry is one of this country's biggest money spinners, and it isn't just about the millions who listen. Imagine how many actually play musical instruments and how much demand there is for guitars, keyboards, studio equipment, drums and other instruments. The fact that people often give up instruments very quickly could ensure a good supply. If you have the know how to advise customers and have a genuine interest in this kind of business, then it shouldn't be long before the musical grapevine has ensure plenty of customers.

Electrical Goods

Electrical goods are where the profits are these days, and it is possible to buy inexpensive second hand goods at low prices and charge a big mark up. Falling into this category are home stereo, hi-fi systems, car stereos, TVs, videos, cameras and other durable household goods such as microwaves, washing machines and refrigerators.

Other Goods

There are other goods you could sell, depending on your specialist knowledge, their availability and shop space. You could consider selling furniture, quality clothing, books or collectables such as stamps, coins, and paintings.

Specialised second hand shops have become standard across the USA, but as yet the idea has not been tried here. Now you have noted the gap in the market and the idea's profit potential why not give it a try? If you can offer quality used and new goods at reasonable prices, in an attractive shop with good service, then it shouldn't be long before customers are beating a path to your door

CHAPTER 53

Correspondence Courses
For Business Opportunities

Fashion Courses

Fashion is something that also greatly appeals to the young, although there are specialist areas that would appeal to all ages, so this course could well be a popular one. You could teach fashion design, how to buy materials and manufacture clothes, plus how to run a fashion business.

Sketching and Cartooning

Although many people admire the skill of artists and cartoonists, very few are able to follow in their footsteps with any degree of competence. Any help they can obtain to help them become better in their chosen pursuit will be welcomed with open arms. Sketching is an increasingly popular pastime and a course covering the basic rules and useful tips to enable beginners to become more competent should get a warm reception. You could offer tips on cartoon drawing and story boarding plus advice on selling their own cartoons. You could even pay a skilled cartoonist to devise the course.

Self Confidence

You could run a course teaching people how to improve their self esteem and confidence. Stress that these are qualities that are vital to impressing job interviewers, enhancing promotion prospects and attracting the opposite sex, and advertise your services in magazines and newspapers.

Beating the System

Offer people the opportunity to shorten the odds when gambling by supplying systems which you know can increase the punter's chance of winning at various games or sports. The course could cover poker, horse racing and various card games.

How to Invest Wisely and Profitably

With traditional safe havens for savings realising pitiful interest returns, a whole new segment of people is looking for ways to make their money work harder. Within this group will be those who are highly cautious, some looking for moderate risk and others who are prepared to speculate in highly volatile markets. What they all need is understandable, jargon free, advice on how the Stock market operates, the rewards and pitfalls to watch out for, and opportunities in foreign markets. You don't have to promise you will find them a fortune - just a monthly focus on a particular sector, with hints for the uninitiated to the knowledgeable, general predictions and possibly tips for them to have a flutter on.

Business Success

If you are now successful in your chosen career after struggling against the odds early on, or if you have dragged a part time venture up by its bootlaces, why not advertise a general blueprint for success so that others can reap the benefit of your experience? There are many people out there who would welcome the know how to solve their current problems, and who better to advise them than someone who has been at the sharp end?

Home Computing

Anyone who has struggled to master their new computer will not need any convincing that the manuals supplied with the systems can send you round the bend. All the more reason for an enterprising person to set up home computer courses for any or all of the popular home computing systems. It is probably best to assume the viewpoint that all new computer users are absolute idiots and need slowly taking by the hand through what seems to them a dense technological haze. There is a mass of computer magazines in which to advertise which should help make this correspondence course a popular and fruitful one.

Tracing Ancestry

It is surprising how many people are deeply interested in this specialist field. The course should cover obtaining information, procedures to follow when researching a family tree, and how to avoid blind alleys. In addition, you could outline procedures for marketing family trees to people with a particular surname and selling personalised family trees.

They say that everyone has a book in them. It is my belief that everyone has a course in them. Valuable information which others can benefit from. All you need to do is find it!

A Few More Ideas

Here are a few more ideas to wet your appetite.
- ☒ language courses
- ☒ knitting
- ☒ needlework
- ☒ making soft toys
- ☒ calligraphy
- ☒ origami
- ☒ film appreciation
- ☒ how to make it in the music business
- ☒ home improvements

☒ biography writing
☒ writing self help books

CHAPTER 54

Counting Your Dough In The CD Swap Shop

The multi-million pound market for compact discs has arisen over the last few years due to their incredible durability and digital clarity giving them a massive advantage over vinyl records and cassettes.

The record shops and CD manufacturers have realised their potential and now the vinyl and cassette formats have been squeezed out in favour of the high priced but cheap to make compact disc.

Why should they get all the profits? CDs could soon be earning you big money if you exploited in the UK a service which has become big in America.

That service is a CD swap shop. Customers simply bring in their unwanted CDs and swap them for something else, paying you a swap fee for the privilege. How many times have you or someone you know bought a CD only to realise one month later that you never play it and are probably unlikely to? By visiting a swap shop it would be possible to exchange it for something that you would listen to, for only a small fee.

You could also price the CDs up for second hand sales in the conventional way, adding an extra dimension to your service. The advantage of CD swapping is that it ensures a constant turnover of cash and stock.

Initially you will need to buy in some stock, so concentrate on stocking popular, well known artists of all genres of music (you could begin to specialise as your stock grows). Currently the average retail price of second hand CDs is around £4, so you could buy these in for £1 or less, and charge a swap fee of £1 or £2.

Considering the country's millions of record buyers, the CD swap shop has a big potential market. By setting up the service you should find that one minute you are selling and swapping CDs and in the next you will be Counting your Dough, and lots of it!

CHAPTER 55

Car Park Sales

You've heard of car boot sales? Well, car park sales are another money making idea, which could help you sell your car and make more money on the side.

They work like this. You book out a car park on one particular day, such as a Sunday or Bank Holiday. You charge a fee to people booking a parking space to display their car for private sale, also charging an admission fee to people coming in to browse for possible bargains. You could even charge commission on any car sold.

In any local newspaper, freesheet or trade magazine such as there are always people advertising second hand cars for sale. Advertise your event in these publications and also put up posters and distribute leaflets advertising the sale, taking care to include the date, time and venue.

You will need to find a suitably sized car park for the sale, checking with the car park owners and the local council that you have permission for the event. You could charge anyone selling their car £20 for a space and set admission prices at £1 per head. If you get 30 car sellers, admit 1560 people in to look around and charge 5% commission on any car sold, then even after car park hire, advertising, telephone and travel expenses, you should be left with a very tidy profit!

BONUS SECTION
Twenty More Great Businesses For You To Think About!

20 IDEAS FOR NOVELTY AND JOKE RELATED PRODUCTS AND SERVICES

Novelty and joke products and services are a serious business. Anyone who lives or works near a seaside resort or tourist attraction will realise this, and the fact is obvious from the number of gift, card, novelty and joke shops situated in any town.

Retailing and manufacturing novelty and joke products are two possibilities, and once you add in mail order and other related businesses it is clear that there are a great number of opportunities in this field.

There are a number of areas in which you could operate. At one end of the process you could make novelty products and sell them on to shops. You could market a product which someone else has made, or involve yourself with the bulk buying and selling of novelty products. By researching the items on sale across the country or even abroad you may discover a demand for a product not already available, so it is possible to set up a business importing and distributing that product.

Alternatively, you could run a gift, joke and novelty shop yourself, run a market stall or even pay someone for the use of a portion of their shop, or simply sell products by mail order. Added to this there are various novelty services you can offer with little or no experience and start up costs required.

The key to success with novelty and joke products and services is originality and humour. The more original the product or service is, and quite often the funnier it is, the more likely it will sell.

These products are also largely linked to fashions and trends, so the more up to date the products are, the better. It is no use selling Bay City Rollers T-shirts for example as today's youth are more likely to demand T-shirts bearing the names of this year's musical craze. Develop an instinct for what items will be consistent sellers and what will only sell for a short period of time. It is far better to get in right at the start of a particular trend rather than when it is dying away, as you will sell more and may even corner the market.

Because a significant proportion of novelty and joke products will be sold as gifts, it is important that the products have a highly personalised element. Most gifts will appeal to a particular market or group of people, so tailor your marketing accordingly.

Here is a list of novelty and joke products and services which you could use to form the basis of a business, either as they are, or modified according to taste or necessity.

Signs

There is a great deal of scope for selling ready made signs that can be displayed in the workplace and in or outside the house. On them could be famous phrases that actors, politicians, writers and other celebrities have used, humorous sayings, insults, proverbs, bible phrases or popular sayings of the moment.

Use your imagination - you could adapt phrases from a book of famous quotations, films, TV programmes or songs. You could make signs for outside the house, such as "My other house is a mansion", or "Trespassers will be eaten", or signs for inside the house such as "Do not disturb - genius at work" or "Keep out - gourmet chef at work", or anything else you can think of.

Making small phrase based signs is an easy process. Once you have your wood it is possible using a hot metal implement to burn or brand on the letters. Alternatively you could carve out the letters, or simply paint them on. By attaching magnets to the back you could sell your signs as fridge magnets. A 'while you wait' sign writing service making simple signs to your customer's specifications is another area to try.

Badges

As well as being cheap and easy to make, badges are a popular and fun product. Designs could feature statements and sayings, celebrities, sporting stars or pop stars. As well as being sold in shops, badges can easily be sold outside pop concerts and sports events, and at tourist sites and festivals.

By cutting out wood in special shapes and hand painting them, a whole range of badges can be created. You could sell animal shaped badges for kids, or badges featuring paintings, statements, symbols and faces. One way to make sure that shops stock your badges is to create an attractive display board for them. Another idea is to sell badges to sports fans along the lines of "I was at XXX match on YYY" in the hope they will collect them in the same way fans collect scarves and programmes.

Because badges are light they are easily sold by mail order and there may also be business opportunities selling badge making equipment. Badges are confusingly called 'buttons' in the USA.

Mugs

A classic novelty and gift item. Mugs can be decorated in a number of ways to target them at a particular trend or a certain type of customer. Mugs featuring the names of people and places, popular cartoon characters, football teams and TV characters are all tried and tested examples of big selling mugs. There may be gaps in the market to try something similar, but try to be original and make sure you are not breaching copyright. Alternatively, make or market a range of fortune telling mugs which could be printed with astrological predictions according to star signs, or feature a guide to reading tea leaves.

Mugs containing opinionated statements could be targeted at a particular market. Examples you could try are "I hate Manchester United" (or any other football team), "I hate work", "I hate Mondays", or on the other hand, "I love my husband/wife/boyfriend/girlfriend" or "I love my job".

Transport Services

Weird and wonderful transport services can be offered in any place where there are a lot of people about, such as a shopping centre, tourist attraction or place of natural beauty. An advantage is that they can often be operated with little or no start up costs or experience. One idea is to operate a sedan chair service. Basically a modified seat with carrying handles, a sedan chair could hold one or two people and be carried by you and one or more helpers for short distances, for a small fee.

Another possibility is to modify a car or build a strange looking go cart to create a novelty taxi, or use a tandem or three wheeled bike to transport people short distances. In places where there are shallow rivers, lakes or ponds you could even charge people to give them piggy back across. It may be necessary to approach your local council to obtain a licence to operate some of these services. This is already happening in London. A crop of trishaw (3-wheeled pedal taxis) has sprung up in theatre land to beat the jams!

Bottled Water

Selling bottled water from famous places is a similar idea to the soil trays. Water from Loch Ness, the River Thames or the Atlantic Ocean, for example, could all be popular. You could market the water as a health product, such as a facial skin care treatment or a therapeutic body soother, but take care that the water is not polluted - try to use water from clean rivers and lakes!

Lucky Charms

Many people are superstitious, meaning there is a big demand for making and selling lucky charms. Four leaf clovers, rabbit feet, horseshoes, destiny dice and number sevens are examples of items which can be sold in shops, by mail order, door to door and on foot.

Hats and Baseball Caps

Hats make excellent joke and novelty items. Possibilities to try out are hats featuring horns, antennae, alien heads, bald heads or the hairstyles of famous people. Australian style cork hats are incredibly easy to make and can be sold as a novelty or functional product. Baseball caps can be bought in bulk very cheaply and printed up according to your target market. Pop stars and rock groups, sports teams and stars, actors and celebrities names, place names and practically anything else can be featured on the caps. Because they are very light and portable the caps can be sold outside pop concerts, sports events, theatres, and at tourist attractions and resorts as well as shops.

Themed Photographs

Taking novelty themed photos is an excellent business idea if you have photographic equipment. You could create humorous painted display boards featuring people wearing bathing costumes, for example, with a hole for people to stick their heads through and be photographed. Alternatively you could buy special outfits for people to wear, such as Victorian clothing, giving the photograph the sepia tinted look typical of the period. You could also hire lookalikes or people dressed in funny outfits, giving people the opportunity to be photographed with the Queen or a real gorilla. These can be very lucrative schemes in places where there are many tourists about.

Garden Products

A business selling novelty seed packets and other garden products could be a fertile source of profit. One idea is to sell packets of garden weeds, such as plants with a strong smell which will have a similar appeal to stink bombs, plants with thorns and spikes, or just ugly looking plants. Novelty plant speech bubble stickers to attach to plant pots featuring phrases such as "My name is XXX, what's yours?", "Fancy a Chat?", or "I like my water shaken, not stirred" is an original idea to try. Small ornamental wishing wells could be made or sold cheaply and have the advantage of not being confined to the garden.

Portable and Indoor Golf Courses

By painting a scaled down golf course onto a white sheet and making plastic or wooden holes and small clubs you can create a mini golf course that can be used in the home, garden or office that is extremely portable and great fun to play on. Similarly, you could create scale versions of well known sports stadiums and motor racing tracks. These can be hired out as well as sold in shops.

Action Painting

An idea which could go down a storm at fairs and public places is to set up an action painting stall. This is where people pay to put on overalls and create their own action painting on a large sheet of paper or material, covering themselves in as much paint as they like and keeping their final picture. The price should include the cost of paint and materials and each person should be set a time limit. The interest such a stall will create should guarantee its success.

Stickers

Another classic joke and novelty product, stickers have the advantage of being relatively easy to print and transport. Stickers targeted at children are likely to sell well, they could feature funny faces, jokes, graffiti, popular phrases and streetwise sayings.

Any product related to children can obviously be sold in toy shops and newsagents as well as gift and joke shops. A range of car stickers could be produced, either along similar lines to the usual stickers seen on cars such as jokes, names and so on, or you could create stickers saying "I hate traffic wardens" or "I hate policemen". Car stickers featuring wartime insignia such as RAF and army crests to stick onto car doors is an original idea you could exploit. Creating a range of amusing party stickers is something else you could try, using phrases like "My name is xxx" "Smile if you fancy me" or "I love your eyes". Ironic travel stickers along the lines of "Fun in the sun at Scunthorpe" or "I spend my holidays at beautiful Milton Keynes" could go down well at holiday gift shops.

Certificates and Licences

Spoof licences and certificates based upon their real equivalents make an excellent joke product. If you have a computer with desktop publishing software they are ideal items to produce cheaply, although printers and photocopy shops will produce them to your specification for a small charge. Joke licences and certificates could feature a space for a name to be filled in, showing that the person is a genius, a dangerous driver, a good husband/wife/mother/father, or anything else you can think of. Novelty educational certificates could show that the holder has a "Diploma in heavy drinking", an "A Level in avoiding the housework", or a "Degree in carnal knowledge".

Sci-fi Products

A market with particular cult appeal, there are any number of science fiction related products you could develop and sell. Sci-fi images like aliens or flying saucers could be created and printed onto products such as T-shirts, badges, mugs, stickers, baseball caps, key fobs, and pens.

You could create messages such as "Beam me anywhere but here", or "I love time travel", or create imaginary deeds to distant stars, space stations or UFO factories. These products lend themselves particularly well to mail order and there are various specialist publications you can advertise in. In addition, gift shops, comic shops and sci-fi conventions are all places at which you could sell your products.

Ashtrays

An interesting concept is to produce a range of ashtrays featuring the faces of well known politicians or celebrities. You actually stub your cigarette out on the faces of people the general public love to hate (or hate to love). In the past this might have included such people as Margaret Thatcher, Jeremy Beadle, or Noel Edmonds, printed on the bottom of the ashtray. Alternatively, you could use football teams, pop groups, or even personal photographs.

Horror Door Hangings

If you have artistic ability, or know someone else who does, a novel idea is to create horror door hangings. A piece of material is painted with an authentic looking horror scene, which is then hung in a doorway. When an unsuspecting person opens the door they are then shocked to be confronted by a ghost, zombie or headless ghoul.

Life Sized Cardboard Celebrities

As the name suggests, the idea is to sell life sized cardboard cut outs of well known celebrities, pop stars or sports stars. Although you may have to obtain permission to use the images of certain people they could make very popular products.

Soft Toys

A consistently big selling item to adults and children alike, the soft toy is something you could either make, or sell and modify according to your market. Everyone has seen the usual selection of toy animals, so why not go for something a little more unusual? Soft toy insects such as bumblebees, caterpillars and ladybirds could have a wide appeal, and cute looking aliens and sea monsters could also be developed. A range of soft toys with particular characteristics could be developed, such as pocket pets, pouch pets, elasticated pets which can be attached to the bedroom ceiling, or velcro pets which stick to clothing.

Joke Books and Cassettes

Publishing themed joke books covering a range of topics could prove a versatile business venture, because in addition to gift shops they can be sold in book shops and other suitable shops. For example, you could produce joke books for a particular town or area, a certain sport or a certain person, or joke books about school, men, women, or pop music. An alternative is to compile these under different headings to produce an encyclopaedia of jokes. Similarly themed cassettes could also be produced, perhaps incorporating humorous songs, rugby and football songs, and drinking songs.

Joke Club

An excellent mail order venture is to set up a joke club, sending out a monthly mail order catalogue of joke and novelty products. You could also write a newsletter including new jokes and ideas, a directory of jokes for different occasions and even include a practical joke of the month. In addition, you could offer a joke writing and finding service.

And There's More

Although we have covered what are perhaps the most exciting, versatile and profitable novelty products and services that could form the basis of a business, there are many others you could try.

Here are a few of them:-

Business cards

Underwear

Condoms

Balloons

Fig leaves

Bubble mix

Pillow cases

Abacuses

Clocks

Voodoo Dolls

Seaweed barometers

Yo yos

Clocks

Bookmarks

Mobiles

Carrier bags

Car stickers

If some of these ideas seem unusual or fanciful, remember you have seen a thousand ideas like this already out there in the shops. If they are in the shops, that means people <u>buy them</u>. If people buy them, <u>someone is making a GREAT profit from selling them</u>! Why can't that 'someone' be YOU?

Made in the USA
Lexington, KY
25 August 2014